SpringerBriefs in Economics

For further volumes:
http://www.springer.com/series/8876

Oscar Bajo-Rubio · Carmen Díaz-Roldán

Macroeconomic Analysis of Monetary Unions

A General Framework Based on the Mundell-Fleming Model

Springer

Prof. Oscar Bajo-Rubio
Department of Economics
Universidad de Castilla-La Mancha
Ronda de Toledo s/n
13071 Ciudad Real
Spain
e-mail: oscar.bajo@uclm.es

Assoc. Prof. Carmen Díaz-Roldán
Department of Economics
Universidad de Castilla-La Mancha
Ronda de Toledo s/n
13071 Ciudad Real
Spain
e-mail: carmen.diazroldan@uclm.es

ISSN 2191-5504 e-ISSN 2191-5512

ISBN 978-3-642-19444-3 e-ISBN 978-3-642-19445-0

DOI 10.1007/978-3-642-19445-0

Springer Heidelberg Dordrecht London New York

Cover design: eStudio Calamar, Berlin/Figueres

Printed on acid-free paper

Springer is part of Springer Science+Business Media (www.springer.com)

Preface

Recent years have seen an increasing interest in the concept of monetary union, i.e., the adoption of a common currency by a group of countries. However, there have been no parallel attempts at a general theoretic analysis of monetary unions. Indeed, open-economy models in macroeconomics textbooks still tend to present the two polar cases of flexible and fixed exchange rates, even though monetary unions are not properly described by either of them. Our purpose, therefore, will be to provide a general framework for the macroeconomic modelling of monetary unions. Specifically, we will adapt an otherwise standard model within the Mundell–Fleming tradition (which represents the reference framework in most textbooks on international macroeconomics), to characterize the workings of a monetary union, a concept pioneered by Robert Mundell himself.

The starting point of the analysis is the standard two-country Mundell–Fleming model with perfect capital mobility, extended to incorporate the supply side in a context of rigid real wages, and modified so that the money market becomes a common one for two countries forming a monetary union. Two versions of the model are presented: one for a small and one for a large monetary union. After solving each model, we derive multipliers for monetary, expenditure, supply, and external shocks, both in the short and the long run; a graphical analysis is also provided. Special attention is paid to the crucial distinction between symmetric and asymmetric shocks.

This book is the result of work done at intervals over several years and in different places. During this time, we have benefited from the financial support of the Spanish Ministries of Education and Science under different projects. We hope that our contribution proves useful to students, teachers, researchers, and anyone interested in macroeconomic modelling.

Contents

Macroeconomic Analysis of Monetary Unions

Abstract Recent years have seen an increasing interest in the concept of monetary union, i.e., the adoption of a common currency by a group of countries. However, there have been no parallel attempts at a general theoretical analysis of monetary unions. In this Brief, we provide a general framework for the macroeconomic modelling of monetary unions, by adapting an otherwise standard model within the Mundell–Fleming tradition, which represents the reference model in most textbooks on international macroeconomics. The starting point of the analysis is the standard two-country Mundell–Fleming model with perfect capital mobility, extended to incorporate the supply side in a context of rigid real wages, and modified so that the money market becomes a common one for two countries forming a monetary union. Two versions of the model are presented: one for a small and one for a large monetary union. After solving each model, we derive multipliers for monetary, expenditure, supply, and external shocks, both in the short and the long run. Special attention is paid to the crucial distinction between symmetric and asymmetric shocks.

Keywords Monetary union · Macroeconomic models · Open economy models · Mundell–Fleming model · Demand side · Supply side · Asymmetric shocks

1 Introduction

The concept of "monetary union" has attracted renewed interest in recent years, as illustrated by the formation in 1999 of the so-called Economic and Monetary Union (EMU) by 12 member countries of the European Union. Since then, EMU has gone through several enlargements, leaving it with a total of 17 member countries at the beginning of 2011. The possibility of advancing towards monetary union is also being discussed in other economically integrated areas, such as

O. Bajo-Rubio and C. Díaz-Roldán, *Macroeconomic Analysis of Monetary Unions*,
SpringerBriefs in Economics, DOI: 10.1007/978-3-642-19445-0_1,

MERCOSUR or NAFTA. An up-to-date survey of the main issues surrounding monetary unification, with particular focus on the European case, can be found in De Grauwe (2009).

Meanwhile, monetary union has been suggested as an alternative to a system of fixed exchange rates. As is well known, some recent experiences (such as the crisis of the European Monetary System in 1992–1993, or the financial crises that affected Mexico and the Southeast Asian countries at the end of 1994 and 1997, respectively) have shown the increasing difficulty for a country to build the reputation that is necessary to sustain a fixed exchange rate system. The ultimate reason is the spectacular growth of world capital markets, following the continuous liberalization and deregulation of capital movements in recent years. Therefore, financial markets' disbelief in a government's commitment to maintaining a certain exchange rate will lead to such massive speculation that central banks will find it extremely difficult to respond. All this has led some authors (e.g., Obstfeld and Rogoff 1995) to suggest that, rather than maintaining a fixed exchange rate, in the near future, countries will face the choice of either maintaining a flexible exchange rate or adopting a common currency with other countries.

However, macroeconomic models of monetary unions are quite infrequent in the literature. Indeed, since monetary unions are not properly described by either a fixed or a flexible exchange rate system, a specific framework is required. The reason is twofold. On the one hand, the formation of a monetary union means the adoption of the same currency by all the countries concerned, which amounts to a fixed exchange rate between the common currency and the old national currencies. On the other hand, however, the exchange rate between the common currency and the currencies of the rest of the world will (usually) be flexible. This is particularly important in relation to country-specific shocks (i.e., those that have an effect on some members of the monetary union, but not on others), which might require a different policy response within each member country of the union (i.e., they might become asymmetric). However, as we will see, the macroeconomic effects of common shocks (i.e., those that have an identical effect on all the members of the monetary union) will coincide with those derived from a conventional model in which the monetary union is taken as a single country.

Our objective will be to develop a general framework for the macroeconomic modelling of monetary unions that could be useful for policy analysis, as well as for teaching purposes. The framework of reference will be a version of the Mundell–Fleming (M–F) model or, more precisely, of the open-economy aggregate demand-aggregate supply (*AD-AS*) model. Despite some recent criticism in academic circles, the M–F model and its extensions remain the framework of reference for most textbooks on international macroeconomics and for applied and policy-oriented research; the ultimate advantage being their great practical usefulness for analyzing economic fluctuations and the effects of policies (Blanchard 1997). To quote Paul Krugman, this 'modified-M–F' model makes up "the workhorse of international-policy analysis" (Krugman 1995, p. 512). Some comprehensive overviews of the M–F model and its extensions are provided by, among others, Dornbusch (1980), Marston (1985) or Frenkel and Razin (1987); for a recent collection of papers using this modelling strategy, see Bajo-Rubio (2003). Furthermore, for the case of a monetary union, Engel (2000) claims to re-examine the optimal currency analysis in an M–F framework.

The literature on optimum currency areas, stemming from the pioneering work of Mundell (1961), stresses the fact that asymmetric shocks (i.e., those requiring a different optimal policy response within each member country) are a potential impediment to the successful working of a monetary union. This is because a common monetary policy cannot be the right tool to cope with asymmetric shocks. For each member country, the formation of a monetary union means, in addition, not only the surrender of monetary policy independence, but also the loss of the exchange rate as a policy instrument. We therefore re-examine the formation of a monetary union in the M–F tradition, by exploring the conditions under which a particular shock can be asymmetric. This also enables us to provide a sort of "closure" of the M–F model, by incorporating the analysis of monetary unions.

As mentioned above, attempts to provide macroeconomic models for monetary unions are not common in the literature; we will refer here to some of them, all based on the M–F model. An early contribution is that of Levin (1983), who develops a model for the analysis of stabilization policy in a currency area, considering only the demand-side of the model. Marston (1984) discusses the choice between a flexible exchange rate and an exchange rate union, following several alternative shocks, in a model that (unlike Levin's) incorporates the supply side. A related analysis is that of Läufer and Sundararajan (1994), who develop a three-country model, in which two countries have a fixed exchange rate, and a flexible exchange rate with the third, to study the international transmission of several economic disturbances (demand-side, monetary, and third-country shocks). A feature common to all these papers is that they consider the case of a small monetary union (or, in the case of Läufer and Sundararajan, two small fixed exchange-rate countries) i.e., the case in which the rest of the world's variables are taken as exogenous.

A very interesting contribution to the modelling of monetary unions is De Bonis (1994), who discusses the effectiveness of monetary and fiscal policies in two alternative models designed, respectively, for a small and a large monetary union (i.e., when the rest of the world's variables are made endogenous). However, the supply-side of the model is not fully specified; and, in particular, price interactions between the union's member countries are omitted for simplicity. In addition, since the analysis of monetary and fiscal policies focuses mainly on their effects on the economy of the union as a whole, the crucial distinction between symmetric and asymmetric shocks is neglected.

More recently, Carlberg (2001) develops a model for a small union, simpler than ours (especially the supply side) under different assumptions on wages (i.e., fixed, flexible, and slow). Using this framework, he examines the effects of several disturbances (monetary and fiscal policies, and labour supply and productivity shocks), both on the union as a whole and on a union made of two countries.

The author next presents a world model, which is simply the small union model where the interest rate is endogenous, and re-examines the effects of the above shocks, also for the world as a whole and for a world made of two regions. Notice that this world model does not compare to our large monetary union case, since the two regions are independent economies. The role of policy coordination in such a framework is further examined in Carlberg (2003).

To summarize, despite the growing (and potentially increasing) importance of monetary unions in the real world, the literature specifically addressing the macroeconomic modelling of monetary unions is rather scant and incomplete in several ways. Hence, our objective here will be to fill this gap, by developing a general framework for the macroeconomic modelling of monetary unions, trying to reconcile realism with tractability. Our ultimate aim is to "close" the M–F model, by incorporating into the basic model the analysis of the formation of a monetary union, a phenomenon of ever-increasing relevance.

The starting point of the analysis will be the standard two-country M–F model with perfect capital mobility (Mundell 1964), extended to incorporate the supply side in a context of rigid real wages (Sachs 1980). This basic open-economy *AD-AS* model will be modified in such a way that the two economies forming the monetary union share a common money market. Two versions of the model will be presented: one for a small monetary union and another for a large one. After solving each model, we will derive monetary, expenditure, supply, and external shocks multipliers, for both the short and long run, paying special attention to the crucial distinction between symmetric and asymmetric shocks.

In particular, we intend to contribute to the existing literature in the following ways:

1. The model has been specifically designed for a monetary union, and the supply side is fully specified.
2. We examine the effects of all possible shocks affecting an economy, namely, monetary, expenditure, supply, and external shocks.
3. The analysis is performed for both the short and the long run, the latter occurring once prices, wages, and the exchange rate fully adjust.
4. We analyze both the case of a small and a large monetary union.
5. We examine the effects of shocks on the member countries of the monetary union, as well as on the union as a whole.
6. An important point in our analysis is that we derive the conditions under which a particular shock becomes asymmetric, i.e., requires a different optimal policy response in each member country. Notice that, since a monetary union would not be well equipped to face this kind of shocks, the higher the probability of asymmetric shocks, the less advisable a monetary union would be.

The basic reference model and the characterization of the shocks are described in Sect. 2. The solution of the model, in terms of the shock multipliers and the graphical analysis, is presented in Sect. 3 for the small monetary union, and in Sect. 4 for the large monetary union. Finally, the main conclusions are summarized in Sect. 5.

2 The Model

2.1 Description of the Model

The model is linear in logs for all the variables (except for the interest and unemployment rates, which denote their levels), Greek letters (all of them standing for positive values) denote the coefficients on the variables, and a star denotes a variable from the rest of the world; time subscripts are omitted for simplicity. Perfect capital mobility is assumed and the exchange rate is flexible.

The demand side of the model is straightforward and given by:

$$y = -\alpha i + \beta(e + p^* - p) + \gamma y^* + f \tag{1}$$

$$m - p = \delta y - \varepsilon i \tag{2}$$

$$i = i^* \tag{3}$$

Equation 1 is the equilibrium condition in the goods market (i.e., the *IS* curve). Real output y depends negatively on the interest rate i; and positively on the real exchange rate $e + p^* - p$, foreign output y^*, and a real, expansionary aggregate demand shock f. In the expression for the real exchange rate, e, p^*, and p denote the nominal exchange rate-defined as the domestic currency price of a unit of foreign currency-, and the foreign and domestic price levels, respectively. Finally, the variable f can include both positive shocks to private consumption or investment, and expansionary fiscal policy changes.

Equation 2 is the equilibrium condition in the money market (i.e., the *LM* curve). Real money balances (with m denoting the nominal money supply) equal the demand for money, which depends positively on real output and negatively on the interest rate. Here, the variable m includes both expansionary monetary policy changes and negative shocks to private money demand; we omit a specific variable for the latter in order to save notation.

Finally, Eq. 3 is the equilibrium condition in the balance of payments under perfect capital mobility, which simply states that domestic and foreign interest rates should be equal.[1]

---

[1] We have preferred to use a simple equation like (3) to represent perfect capital mobility, as in most textbook presentations of the M–F model. Modifying the right-hand side to include the expected rate of depreciation would complicate the multipliers without altering the long-run results, and simply delays the adjustment of aggregate demand to the exchange rate in the short run. In particular, for the case of the small monetary union, a country-specific expenditure shock would have an ambiguous effect in the short run on the partner's output and prices, and a positive effect on those of the union. In turn, a common expenditure shock or a positive shock to the trade balance would have a positive effect on the union's output and prices (results available from the authors upon request).

Turning to aggregate supply, we follow the now standard framework of Layard et al. (1991). The supply side of the model includes a wage equation, a price equation, and a relationship between output and employment[2]:

$$w = p_C^E - \phi u + \varphi prod + z^w \tag{4}$$

$$p = w - \varphi prod + z^p \tag{5}$$

$$n = y - prod \tag{6}$$

Equation 4 shows, first, that the nominal wage w is fully indexed to the expected value of the consumer price index p_C^E. Thus, this expected real wage depends negatively on the unemployment rate u; and positively on labour productivity *prod*, and some wage pressure factors summarized in z^w.

Equation 5 sets prices as a markup over average variable costs, where the only variable factor is labour. The markup covers any fixed costs, and is assumed to depend on the variables summarized in z^p.

Finally, Eq. 6 defines employment n, as the difference between real output and productivity.

As regards price expectations, our assumption of nominal inertia means that it takes some time for prices and wages to adjust to a shock. Specifically, expectations on the consumer price index p_C are given by:

$$p_C^E = p_{C,-1} \tag{7}$$

where the subscript –1 denotes the value of a variable at the beginning of the period of analysis.[3] This kind of assumption is common in many macroeconomics textbooks [see, e.g., Blanchard (2009), Carlin and Soskice (2006), or Mankiw (2010)], and will allow us to separate the short- and long-run effects of shocks, the latter occurring when prices and wages fully adjust. This specification of expectations appears to be consistent with the standard stylized facts about the dynamic effects of monetary policy (Mankiw 2000). As noticed by Ball (2000), such backward-looking expectations can be interpreted as a "near-rational rule of thumb" in the sense of Akerlof and Yellen (1985), given the costs of gathering and processing the information needed for fully rational inflation forecasts; see also Rudd and Whelan (2006).

To complete the supply side of the model, two definitions are required. The first is the consumer price index, which is a weighted average of domestic and foreign prices, with the latter denominated in domestic currency:

[2] As usual, the coefficients on the variable *prod* are the same in the wage and price equations in order to prevent a long-run effect of productivity on unemployment; see Layard et al. (1991).

[3] Notice that this assumption would lead to the further assumption of zero expectations for future inflation, which would mean in turn that the interest rate i in (1) would stand both for the real and the nominal interest rate. Alternatively, changes in inflation expectations might be reflected in the shock f.

$$p_C = \overline{\sigma}p + (1 - \overline{\sigma})(p^* + e) \tag{8}$$

where $\overline{\sigma} > 0$ denotes the weight of domestic prices. The second is the rate of unemployment, that is, the difference between labour force l and employment:

$$u = l - n \tag{9}$$

Now, from (4) to (9), we can derive the equation for aggregate supply:

$$y = \frac{1}{\phi}p - \frac{\overline{\sigma}}{\phi}p_{-1} - \frac{(1 - \overline{\sigma})}{\phi}(p^*_{-1} + e_{-1}) - s \tag{10}$$

where s is a contractionary supply shock capturing all the possible supply shocks considered above (i.e., pressures on prices and wages, and shocks to labour force and productivity):

$$s = \frac{z^p + z^w}{\phi} - l - prod$$

In turn, the long-run aggregate supply equation is given by:

$$y = -\frac{(1 - \overline{\sigma})}{\phi}(p^* + e - p) - s \tag{10'}$$

In this way, our basic model is made up of Eqs. 1–3, and 10 for the short run; and Eqs. 1–3, and 10′ for the long run. As noted earlier, the advantage of this specification is that it will allow separate examination of the immediate or impact effect of a shock, and its final effect, once prices and wages have adjusted to the new equilibrium, and there are no exchange-rate expectation errors.

2.2 A Macroeconomic Model for a Monetary Union

Next, we will assume that, rather than a single country, the above model describes a monetary union. We define a monetary union as a group of countries that have decided to abolish their national currencies to adopt a new currency, common to all of them, assuming a flexible exchange rate with the rest of the world. Under the framework developed in the previous section, every equation in the monetary union model can be written in terms of every member country, unlike the money market equilibrium equation, which is now common to all of them.

To keep things as simple as possible, we will assume that the monetary union is made up of two identical countries, denoted by the subscripts 1 and 2; and that each variable of the union is a weighted average of the corresponding variables of countries 1 and 2, with the weights equal to $\frac{1}{2}$. Specifically, for any variable x:

$$x = \frac{1}{2}(x_1 + x_2)$$

We will make the additional assumption that, the consumption price index of each member country is defined such that its own prices have greater weight than those of the other country. In terms of Eq. 8: $\overline{\sigma} = \sigma + \sigma'$, $\sigma > \sigma'$, so that:

$$p_{C1} = \sigma p_1 + \sigma' p_2 + (1 - \sigma - \sigma')(p^* + e)$$

$$p_{C2} = \sigma p_2 + \sigma' p_1 + (1 - \sigma - \sigma')(p^* + e)$$

Hence, we can write the union's Eqs. 1, 2, and 10 for countries 1 and 2. In this way, the model for the two countries of the monetary union will be given by:

$$y_1 = -\alpha i^* + \beta(e + p^* - p_1) + \beta(p_2 - p_1) + \gamma y^* + \gamma(y_2 - y_1) + f_1 \quad (11)$$

$$y_2 = -\alpha i^* + \beta(e + p^* - p_2) + \beta(p_1 - p_2) + \gamma y^* + \gamma(y_1 - y_2) + f_2 \quad (12)$$

$$m - \frac{1}{2}(p_1 + p_2) = \frac{\delta}{2}(y_1 + y_2) - \varepsilon i^* \quad (13)$$

$$y_1 = \frac{1}{\phi} p_1 - \frac{\sigma}{\phi} p_{1,-1} - \frac{\sigma'}{\phi} p_{2,-1} - \frac{(1 - \sigma - \sigma')}{\phi}(p^*_{-1} + e_{-1}) - s_1 \quad (14)$$

$$y_2 = \frac{1}{\phi} p_2 - \frac{\sigma}{\phi} p_{2,-1} - \frac{\sigma'}{\phi} p_{1,-1} - \frac{(1 - \sigma - \sigma')}{\phi}(p^*_{-1} + e_{-1}) - s_2 \quad (15)$$

where, in the long run, once prices and wages have fully adjusted, Eqs. 14 and 15 should be replaced by:

$$y_1 = \frac{(1 - \sigma)}{\phi} p_1 - \frac{\sigma'}{\phi} p_2 - \frac{(1 - \sigma - \sigma')}{\phi}(p^* + e) - s_1 \quad (14')$$

$$y_2 = \frac{(1 - \sigma)}{\phi} p_2 - \frac{\sigma'}{\phi} p_1 - \frac{(1 - \sigma - \sigma')}{\phi}(p^* + e) - s_2 \quad (15')$$

Recall that, in the equations above, the foreign interest rate i^* has already replaced the domestic interest rate in (1) and (2), according to Eq. 3; and that $s_1 = \frac{z_1^p + z_1^w}{\phi} - l_1 - prod_1$, $s_2 = \frac{z_2^p + z_2^w}{\phi} - l_2 - prod_2$.

In the model above, Eqs. 11 and 12 are the equilibrium conditions in the goods markets of countries 1 and 2. Real output of each member country of the union depends negatively on the union's interest rate; and positively on the real exchange rate with the rest of the world, relative prices versus the other country, foreign output, the output of the other country (relative to its own output),[4] and a

---

[4] Notice that the introduction of the terms $(y_2 - y_1)$ and $(y_1 - y_2)$ on the right-hand side of Eqs. 11 and 12 is simply a convenient device enabling us to maintain the parameters of the monetary union model, and facilitate derivation of the multipliers below. Notice also that relative prices $(p_2 - p_1)$ and $(p_1 - p_2)$ are equivalent to the real exchange rate with the other member country, once monetary union removes the nominal exchange rate between them.

real, expansionary aggregate demand shock. In turn, Eq. 13 is the equilibrium condition in the common money market of the union, where m denotes the nominal money supply of the union, managed by the union's common central bank; as well as any negative shocks to private money demand, which are also common to both countries in a monetary union. Finally, Eqs. 14 and 15 are the supply functions of countries 1 and 2, so that real output depends on the price level, the different components of the (expected) consumption price index, and a contractionary supply shock.

As can be easily proved, from the weighted sum of Eqs. 11 and 12, we can obtain Eq. 1, with i replaced, from (3); and, from the weighted sum of Eqs. 14 and 15, we can obtain Eq. 10. In turn, Eq. 13 is a transformation of Eq. 2, with i replaced from (3).

Taking the rest of the world's variables (y^*, p^*, and i^*) to be exogenous, the model given by Eqs. 11–15 represents a *small monetary union*. This is the case when, as in the small open economy, the union is so small that is unable to affect the economic conditions of the rest of the world. The model of the small monetary union has five endogenous variables: y_1, y_2, p_1, p_2, and e; the whole set of equations is shown in Table 1.

However, we could alternatively assume that the union is large enough to influence the economic conditions of the rest of the world. This would be the case of a *large monetary union*, where the rest of the world's variables become endogenous, so that the economy of the rest of the world should be explicitly modelled.

Assuming an analogous framework to that of the union, we can write the equations equivalent to (1), (2), and (10) for the rest of the world as:

$$y^* = -\alpha i^* - \beta(e + p^* - p) + \gamma y + f^*$$

$$m^* - p^* = \delta y^* - \varepsilon i^*$$

Table 1 The model for a small monetary union

Short run	
$y_1 = -\alpha i^* + \beta(e + p^* - p_1) + \beta(p_2 - p_1) + \gamma y^* + \gamma(y_2 - y_1) + f_1$	(11)
$y_2 = -\alpha i^* + \beta(e + p^* - p_2) + \beta(p_1 - p_2) + \gamma y^* + \gamma(y_1 - y_2) + f_2$	(12)
$m - \frac{1}{2}(p_1 + p_2) = \frac{\delta}{2}(y_1 + y_2) - \varepsilon i^*$	(13)
$y_1 = \frac{1}{\phi}p_1 - \frac{\sigma}{\phi}p_{1,-1} - \frac{\sigma'}{\phi}p_{2,-1} - \frac{(1-\sigma-\sigma')}{\phi}(p^*_{-1} + e_{-1}) - s_1$	(14)
$y_2 = \frac{1}{\phi}p_2 - \frac{\sigma}{\phi}p_{2,-1} - \frac{\sigma'}{\phi}p_{1,-1} - \frac{(1-\sigma-\sigma')}{\phi}(p^*_{-1} + e_{-1}) - s_2$	(15)
Long run	
$y_1 = -\alpha i^* + \beta(e + p^* - p_1) + \beta(p_2 - p_1) + \gamma y^* + \gamma(y_2 - y_1) + f_1$	(11)
$y_2 = -\alpha i^* + \beta(e + p^* - p_2) + \beta(p_1 - p_2) + \gamma y^* + \gamma(y_1 - y_2) + f_2$	(12)
$m - \frac{1}{2}(p_1 + p_2) = \frac{\delta}{2}(y_1 + y_2) - \varepsilon i^*$	(13)
$y_1 = \frac{(1-\sigma)}{\phi}p_1 - \frac{\sigma'}{\phi}p_2 - \frac{(1-\sigma-\sigma')}{\phi}(p^* + e) - s_1$	(14′)
$y_2 = \frac{(1-\sigma)}{\phi}p_2 - \frac{\sigma'}{\phi}p_1 - \frac{(1-\sigma-\sigma')}{\phi}(p^* + e) - s_2$	(15′)

Note The endogenous variables are y_1, y_2, p_1, p_2, e

$$y^* = \frac{1}{\phi}p^* - \frac{\overline{\sigma}}{\phi}p^*_{-1} - \frac{(1-\overline{\sigma})}{\phi}(p_{-1} - e_{-1}) - s^*$$

where the latter is obtained from the set of equations equivalent to (4) to (9) for the rest of the world. As before, f^* is a real, expansionary aggregate demand shock, m^* is the nominal money supply of the rest of the world (including also negative shocks to private money demand), and $s^* = \frac{z^{p*}+z^{w*}}{\phi} - l^* - prod^*$ is a contractionary supply shock (bringing together the effects of pressures on prices and wages, and labour force and productivity shocks). When the monetary union variables are written in terms of countries 1 and 2 (recalling that $\overline{\sigma} = \sigma + \sigma'$, $\sigma > \sigma'$), the equations for the rest of the world become:

$$y^* = -\alpha i^* - \beta(e + p^*) + \frac{\beta}{2}(p_1 + p_2) + \frac{\gamma}{2}(y_1 + y_2) + f^* \tag{16}$$

$$m^* - p^* = \delta y^* - \varepsilon i^* \tag{17}$$

$$y^* = \frac{1}{\phi}p^* - \frac{(\sigma+\sigma')}{\phi}p^*_{-1} - \frac{(1-\sigma-\sigma')}{2\phi}(p_{1,-1} + p_{2,-1}) + \frac{(1-\sigma-\sigma')}{\phi}e_{-1} - s^* \tag{18}$$

with Eq. 18 replaced in the long run by:

$$y^* = \frac{(1-\sigma-\sigma')}{\phi}(p^* + e) - \frac{(1-\sigma-\sigma')}{2\phi}(p_1 + p_2) - s^* \tag{18'}$$

Thus, the large monetary union model is given by Eqs. 11–18, with eight endogenous variables: y_1, y_2, p_1, p_2, e, y^*, p^*, and i^*. The whole set of equations for the large monetary union model is shown in Table 2.

2.3 *Characterization of the Shocks*

In the next section, we examine the effects of different shocks on the endogenous variables of the model presented above. Hence, in what follows, we need to characterize the kind of shocks to be analyzed.

From the perspective of the monetary union, shocks will be characterized according to three criteria:

(a) Whether the shock occurs in the money market, the goods market, the supply side, or the rest of the world; i.e., whether it is a *monetary* shock, an *expenditure* (or aggregate demand) shock, a *supply* shock, or an *external* shock, respectively.
(b) Whether the shock occurs simultaneously in all member countries of the monetary union or in only one of them, i.e., whether it is (in origin) a *common* shock or a *country-specific* shock.

Table 2 The model for a large monetary union

Short run

$$y_1 = -\alpha i^* + \beta(e + p^* - p_1) + \beta(p_2 - p_1) + \gamma y^* + \gamma(y_2 - y_1) + f_1 \quad (11)$$

$$y_2 = -\alpha i^* + \beta(e + p^* - p_2) + \beta(p_1 - p_2) + \gamma y^* + \gamma(y_1 - y_2) + f_2 \quad (12)$$

$$m - \tfrac{1}{2}(p_1 + p_2) = \tfrac{\delta}{2}(y_1 + y_2) - \varepsilon i^* \quad (13)$$

$$y_1 = \tfrac{1}{\phi}p_1 - \tfrac{\sigma}{\phi}p_{1,-1} - \tfrac{\sigma'}{\phi}p_{2,-1} - \tfrac{(1-\sigma-\sigma')}{\phi}(p^*_{-1} + e_{-1}) - s_1 \quad (14)$$

$$y_2 = \tfrac{1}{\phi}p_2 - \tfrac{\sigma}{\phi}p_{2,-1} - \tfrac{\sigma'}{\phi}p_{1,-1} - \tfrac{(1-\sigma-\sigma')}{\phi}(p^*_{-1} + e_{-1}) - s_2 \quad (15)$$

$$y^* = -\alpha i^* - \beta(e + p^*) + \tfrac{\beta}{2}(p_1 + p_2) + \tfrac{\gamma}{2}(y_1 + y_2) + f^* \quad (16)$$

$$m^* - p^* = \delta y^* - \varepsilon i^* \quad (17)$$

$$y^* = \tfrac{1}{\phi}p^* - \tfrac{(\sigma+\sigma')}{\phi}p^*_{-1} - \tfrac{(1-\sigma-\sigma')}{2\phi}(p_{1,-1} + p_{2,-1}) + \tfrac{(1-\sigma-\sigma')}{\phi}e_{-1} - s^* \quad (18)$$

Long run

$$y_1 = -\alpha i^* + \beta(e + p^* - p_1) + \beta(p_2 - p_1) + \gamma y^* + \gamma(y_2 - y_1) + f_1 \quad (11)$$

$$y_2 = -\alpha i^* + \beta(e + p^* - p_2) + \beta(p_1 - p_2) + \gamma y^* + \gamma(y_1 - y_2) + f_2 \quad (12)$$

$$m - \tfrac{1}{2}(p_1 + p_2) = \tfrac{\delta}{2}(y_1 + y_2) - \varepsilon i^* \quad (13)$$

$$y_1 = \tfrac{(1-\sigma)}{\phi}p_1 - \tfrac{\sigma'}{\phi}p_2 - \tfrac{(1-\sigma-\sigma')}{\phi}(p^* + e) - s_1 \quad (14')$$

$$y_2 = \tfrac{(1-\sigma)}{\phi}p_2 - \tfrac{\sigma'}{\phi}p_1 - \tfrac{(1-\sigma-\sigma')}{\phi}(p^* + e) - s_2 \quad (15')$$

$$y^* = -\alpha i^* - \beta(e + p^*) + \tfrac{\beta}{2}(p_1 + p_2) + \tfrac{\gamma}{2}(y_1 + y_2) + f^* \quad (16)$$

$$m^* - p^* = \delta y^* - \varepsilon i^* \quad (17)$$

$$y^* = \tfrac{(1-\sigma-\sigma')}{\phi}(p^* + e) - \tfrac{(1-\sigma-\sigma')}{2\phi}(p_1 + p_2) - s^* \quad (18')$$

Note The endogenous variables are y_1, y_2, p_1, p_2, e, y^*, p^*, i^*

(c) Whether the shock requires the same optimal policy response in every member country of the union or a different one in each, i.e., whether it is a *symmetric* shock or an *asymmetric* shock.

In this classification, monetary shocks include monetary policy actions, and shocks to private money demand. Expenditure shocks include fiscal policy actions, and shocks to private consumption and investment. In turn, supply shocks include pressures on prices and wages, and shocks to labour force and productivity. Finally, external shocks include external output, price, and interest rate shocks, in the case of a small monetary union; and external monetary, expenditure, and supply shocks, in the case of a large monetary union.

Furthermore, according to the definition above, monetary and external shocks will be always common to the whole monetary union, while expenditure and supply shocks could either be common to the whole monetary union or specific to a particular country.

Note that, in strict terms, country-specific monetary shocks affecting the demand for money in a single member country of the union are a possibility (remember that, in a monetary union, money supply is commonly determined). However, it can be shown that this kind of shock would have the same impact on both countries and on the union as a whole, and half the impact of a (common) money supply shock. The ultimate reason for this is that the money market is common to all the member countries; in other words, what was originally a country-specific money demand shock would in practice have the effect of a common shock. Although one can also imagine external shocks having an unequal impact on the goods produced in each member country of the union; such shocks, would in practice have the effect of country-specific expenditure shocks. Therefore, we will maintain our simplifying assumption that monetary and external shocks can always be characterized as common shocks.

A common shock will have the same effect on every member country of the union, and thus require the same policy response within each of them, which means that common shocks will always be symmetric. However, a country-specific shock will have a different effect in the country of origin of the shock than in the other member country to which the shock is transmitted. In particular, the effect of a country-specific shock can be transmitted to the other country either with the same sign, as in the so-called "locomotive" effect; or with the opposite sign, as in the "beggar-thy-neighbour" effect. The result depends on the relative strength of the transmission channel: aggregate demand in the case of the "locomotive" effect, and the interest rate and the real exchange rate, in that of the "beggar-thy-neighbour" effect. Under the "locomotive" effect, country-specific shocks will again require the same policy response in every country, and will therefore be symmetric; under the "beggar-thy-neighbour" effect, on the other hand, country-specific shocks will require a different policy response in each country, and will therefore be asymmetric.

Next, we introduce some terminology. In general, for any source of disturbance d, a shock will be denoted as:

- $\Delta d \neq 0$, when common
- $\Delta d_1 \neq 0, \quad \Delta d_2 = 0$, when country-specific, originating in country 1
- $\Delta d_1 = 0, \quad \Delta d_2 \neq 0$, when country-specific, originating in country 2

where $d = \frac{d_1+d_2}{2}$. For the sake of simplicity, we will always consider only the case of positively signed shocks, thus omitting negatively-signed shocks, which are analogous. The shocks to be analyzed are as follows:

1. Monetary shocks, as $\Delta m > 0$ (reflecting either an increase in the union's money supply, or a decrease in private money demand within the monetary union).
2. Expenditure shocks, as $\Delta f_1 > 0$ or $\Delta f_2 > 0$ if country-specific, or $\Delta f > 0$ if common (reflecting either a higher government deficit, or an exogenous increase in private consumption or investment within the monetary union).
3. Supply shocks, as $\Delta s_1 > 0$ or $\Delta s_2 > 0$ if country-specific, or $\Delta s > 0$ if common (reflecting either an exogenous increase in prices or wages, or a fall in the labour force or productivity within the monetary union).
4. External shocks, as $\Delta y^* > 0$, $\Delta p^* > 0$, or $\Delta i^* > 0$, for the case of a small monetary union (reflecting either a positive shock to the trade balance through higher foreign output or prices, or a negative shock to capital movements through a higher foreign interest rate). Or, alternatively, as $\Delta m^* > 0$, $\Delta f^* > 0$, or $\Delta s^* > 0$, for the case of a large monetary union (reflecting either an

expansionary foreign monetary shock, an expansionary foreign expenditure shock, or a contractionary foreign supply shock).

The different sources of shocks characterized above are summarized schematically below:

$$\text{shocks}\begin{cases}\text{symmetric}\begin{cases}\text{common}: m, f, s, \text{external}\\ \text{country--specific, ``locomotive''}: f_i, s_i\ (i=1,2)\end{cases}\\ \\ \text{asymmetric}\{\text{country--specific, ``beggar--thy--neighbor''}: f_i, s_i\ (i=1,2)\end{cases}$$

As mentioned earlier, the effect of a common shock will be the same for every member country of the union; thus, for the output level, for example, we would have:

$$\frac{\partial y_1}{\partial d} = \frac{\partial y_2}{\partial d}$$

for $d = m, f, s$, external shocks. In turn, the effect on the union as a whole will be the weighted sum of the effect on each member country, and hence equal to the effect on each one:

$$\frac{\partial y}{\partial d} = \frac{1}{2}\left(\frac{\partial y_1}{\partial d} + \frac{\partial y_2}{\partial d}\right) = \frac{\partial y_1}{\partial d} = \frac{\partial y_2}{\partial d}$$

Country-specific shocks will have the same effect on the country of origin of the shock, regardless of the country; that is:

$$\frac{\partial y_1}{\partial d_1} = \frac{\partial y_2}{\partial d_2}$$

for $d_i = f_i, s_i$ $(i = 1, 2)$. The effect on the country to which the shock is transmitted will be also the same, regardless of the country:

$$\frac{\partial y_2}{\partial d_1} = \frac{\partial y_1}{\partial d_2}$$

and will be smaller in size, in absolute terms, than in the country of origin of the shock:

$$\left|\frac{\partial y_2}{\partial d_1}\right| < \left|\frac{\partial y_1}{\partial d_1}\right|, \quad \left|\frac{\partial y_1}{\partial d_2}\right| < \left|\frac{\partial y_2}{\partial d_2}\right|$$

Recall that the sign can be the same or the opposite, depending on whether the "locomotive" or the "beggar-thy-neighbour" effect prevails (or, in other words, depending on whether the shock is symmetric or asymmetric).

Finally, the effect on the union as a whole will again be the weighted sum of the effect on each member country:

$$\frac{\partial y}{\partial d_1} = \frac{1}{2}\left(\frac{\partial y_1}{\partial d_1} + \frac{\partial y_2}{\partial d_1}\right) = \frac{1}{2}\left(\frac{\partial y_1}{\partial d_2} + \frac{\partial y_2}{\partial d_2}\right) = \frac{\partial y}{\partial d_2}$$

which, in turn, will be the same regardless of the country of origin of the shock. Following from our assumption of perfectly identical countries, the effect of a country-specific shock on the union as a whole will have the same sign as in the country of origin. The effect on the union as a whole will be greater, in absolute terms, than half the effect on the country of origin, in the "locomotive" effect case; and smaller, in absolute terms, than half the effect on the country of origin, in the "beggar-thy-neighbour" case.

To conclude, notice that the above results for country-specific shocks can change if the member countries of the union are not perfectly identical. In general, the higher the receiving country's share in the union, the less the effect of the shock on the union as a whole, so that:

- If the "locomotive" effect prevails, the effect of the shock on the union as a whole will have the same sign as in the country of origin; and will be greater, in absolute terms, than the effect on that country weighted by its share in the union.
- If the shock is of the "beggar-thy-neighbour" type, and the country of origin has more than a 50% share in the union, the effect on the union as a whole will still have the same sign; but will be lower in absolute value.
- If the shock is of the "beggar-thy-neighbour" type, and the country of origin has less than a 50% share in the union, the effect on the union as a whole will have the opposite sign.

In the next two sections, we analyze the effects of the different shocks examined above, on the endogenous variables of the two models developed in this section, that is, those describing a small and a large monetary union, respectively. As in Sargent (1979), we will find reduced forms for the endogenous variables as a function of the shocks, and then obtain their multipliers, i.e., partial derivatives of the endogenous variables with respect to the shocks. Notice that, since our models are linear in logs, these multipliers will represent elasticities. For the sake of simplicity, we show only the signs of the multipliers; the detailed solutions of the two models can be found in the Appendix. A graphical analysis is also provided.

3 The Model for a Small Monetary Union

3.1 Shock Multipliers

The model for a small monetary union, shown in Table 1, is made up of Eqs. 11–15, with five endogenous variables: y_1, y_2, p_1, p_2, and e. Recall that, in this case, the rest of the world's variables (y^*, p^*, and i^*) are exogenous to the model. We first show the short-run multipliers, obtained after solving the model given by Eqs. 11–15; and then the long-run multipliers, obtained from the solution of the long-run version of the model, i.e., that given by Eqs. 11–13, 14′ and 15′. A summary of the results is presented in Table 3.

Table 3 Effects of shocks: small monetary union

		Effects on						
		Output			Prices			Exchange rate
A. Common shocks ($d \neq 0$)								
Shocks		$\frac{\partial y_1}{\partial d} = \frac{\partial y_2}{\partial d} = \frac{\partial y}{\partial d}$			$\frac{\partial p_1}{\partial d} = \frac{\partial p_2}{\partial d} = \frac{\partial p}{\partial d}$			$\frac{\partial e}{\partial d}$
Monetary	sr	+			+			+
m	lr	0			1			1
Expenditure	sr	0			0			–
f	lr	+			–			–
Supply	sr = lr	–			+			±
s								
Foreign output	sr	0			0			–
y^*	lr	+			–			–
Foreign prices	sr=lr	0			0			−1
p^*								
Foreign interest rate	sr	+			+			+
i^*	lr	–			+			+
B. Country-specific shocks ($d_i \neq 0,\ d_j = 0$)								
Shocks		$\frac{\partial y_1}{\partial d_1} = \frac{\partial y_2}{\partial d_2}$	$\frac{\partial y_2}{\partial d_1} = \frac{\partial y_1}{\partial d_2}$	$\frac{\partial y}{\partial d_1} = \frac{\partial y}{\partial d_2}$	$\frac{\partial p_1}{\partial d_1} = \frac{\partial p_2}{\partial d_2}$	$\frac{\partial p_2}{\partial d_1} = \frac{\partial p_1}{\partial d_2}$	$\frac{\partial p}{\partial d_1} = \frac{\partial p}{\partial d_2}$	$\frac{\partial e}{\partial d_1} = \frac{\partial e}{\partial d_2}$
Expenditure	sr	+	–	0	+	–	0	–
f_1, f_2	lr	+	±	+	±	–	–	–
Supply	sr = lr	–	±	–	+	±	+	±
s_1, s_2								

Notes (i) sr = short run, lr = long run
(ii) $d = m, f, s, y^*, p^*, i^*$
(iii) $d_i, d_j = f_i, f_j, s_i, s_j$ $(i, j = 1, 2)$

The signs of the multipliers, for the different shocks analyzed, are:

(A) Monetary shocks

$$\frac{\partial y_1}{\partial m}=\frac{\partial y_2}{\partial m}=\frac{\partial y}{\partial m}>0,\ \frac{\partial p_1}{\partial m}=\frac{\partial p_2}{\partial m}=\frac{\partial p}{\partial m}>0,\ \frac{\partial e}{\partial m}>0$$

in the short run, and

$$\frac{\partial y_1}{\partial m}=\frac{\partial y_2}{\partial m}=\frac{\partial y}{\partial m}=0,\ \frac{\partial p_1}{\partial m}=\frac{\partial p_2}{\partial m}=\frac{\partial p}{\partial m}=1,\ \frac{\partial e}{\partial m}=1$$

in the long run.

(B) Expenditure shocks

(B.1) Country-specific expenditure shocks

$$\frac{\partial y_1}{\partial f_1}=\frac{\partial y_2}{\partial f_2}>0,\ \frac{\partial y_2}{\partial f_1}=\frac{\partial y_1}{\partial f_2}<0,\ \frac{\partial y}{\partial f_1}=\frac{\partial y}{\partial f_2}=0$$

$$\frac{\partial p_1}{\partial f_1}=\frac{\partial p_2}{\partial f_2}>0,\ \frac{\partial p_2}{\partial f_1}=\frac{\partial p_1}{\partial f_2}<0,\ \frac{\partial p}{\partial f_1}=\frac{\partial p}{\partial f_2}=0$$

$$\frac{\partial e}{\partial f_1}=\frac{\partial e}{\partial f_2}<0$$

in the short run, and

$$\frac{\partial y_1}{\partial f_1}=\frac{\partial y_2}{\partial f_2}>0,\ \frac{\partial y_2}{\partial f_1}=\frac{\partial y_1}{\partial f_2}\lesseqgtr 0,\ \frac{\partial y}{\partial f_1}=\frac{\partial y}{\partial f_2}>0$$

$$\frac{\partial p_1}{\partial f_1}=\frac{\partial p_2}{\partial f_2}\lesseqgtr 0,\ \frac{\partial p_2}{\partial f_1}=\frac{\partial p_1}{\partial f_2}<0,\ \frac{\partial p}{\partial f_1}=\frac{\partial p}{\partial f_2}<0$$

$$\frac{\partial e}{\partial f_1}=\frac{\partial e}{\partial f_2}<0$$

in the long run.

(B.2) Common expenditure shocks

$$\frac{\partial y_1}{\partial f}=\frac{\partial y_2}{\partial f}=\frac{\partial y}{\partial f}=\frac{\partial p_1}{\partial f}=\frac{\partial p_2}{\partial f}=\frac{\partial p}{\partial f}=0,\ \frac{\partial e}{\partial f}<0$$

in the short run, and

$$\frac{\partial y_1}{\partial f}=\frac{\partial y_2}{\partial f}=\frac{\partial y}{\partial f}>0,\ \frac{\partial p_1}{\partial f}=\frac{\partial p_2}{\partial f}=\frac{\partial p}{\partial f}<0,\ \frac{\partial e}{\partial f}<0$$

in the long run.

(C) Supply shocks

(C.1) Country-specific supply shocks

$$\frac{\partial y_1}{\partial s_1} = \frac{\partial y_2}{\partial s_2} < 0, \; \frac{\partial y_2}{\partial s_1} = \frac{\partial y_1}{\partial s_2} \lesseqgtr 0, \; \frac{\partial y}{\partial s_1} = \frac{\partial y}{\partial s_2} < 0$$

$$\frac{\partial p_1}{\partial s_1} = \frac{\partial p_2}{\partial s_2} > 0, \; \frac{\partial p_2}{\partial s_1} = \frac{\partial p_1}{\partial s_2} \lesseqgtr 0, \; \frac{\partial p}{\partial s_1} = \frac{\partial p}{\partial s_2} > 0$$

$$\frac{\partial e}{\partial s_1} = \frac{\partial e}{\partial s_2} \lesseqgtr 0$$

both in the short run and in the long run.

(C.2) Common supply shocks

$$\frac{\partial y_1}{\partial s} = \frac{\partial y_2}{\partial s} = \frac{\partial y}{\partial s} < 0, \; \frac{\partial p_1}{\partial s} = \frac{\partial p_2}{\partial s} = \frac{\partial p}{\partial s} > 0, \; \frac{\partial e}{\partial s} \lesseqgtr 0$$

both in the short run and in the long run.

(D) External shocks

(D.1) Foreign output shocks

$$\frac{\partial y_1}{\partial y^*} = \frac{\partial y_2}{\partial y^*} = \frac{\partial y}{\partial y^*} = \frac{\partial p_1}{\partial y^*} = \frac{\partial p_2}{\partial y^*} = \frac{\partial p}{\partial y^*} = 0, \; \frac{\partial e}{\partial y^*} < 0$$

in the short run, and

$$\frac{\partial y_1}{\partial y^*} = \frac{\partial y_2}{\partial y^*} = \frac{\partial y}{\partial y^*} > 0, \; \frac{\partial p_1}{\partial y^*} = \frac{\partial p_2}{\partial y^*} = \frac{\partial p}{\partial y^*} < 0, \; \frac{\partial e}{\partial y^*} < 0$$

in the long run.

(D.2) Foreign price shocks

$$\frac{\partial y_1}{\partial p^*} = \frac{\partial y_2}{\partial p^*} = \frac{\partial y}{\partial p^*} = \frac{\partial p_1}{\partial p^*} = \frac{\partial p_2}{\partial p^*} = \frac{\partial p}{\partial p^*} = 0, \; \frac{\partial e}{\partial p^*} = -1$$

both in the short run and in the long run.

(D.3) Foreign interest rate shocks

$$\frac{\partial y_1}{\partial i^*} = \frac{\partial y_2}{\partial i^*} = \frac{\partial y}{\partial i^*} > 0, \; \frac{\partial p_1}{\partial i^*} = \frac{\partial p_2}{\partial i^*} = \frac{\partial p}{\partial i^*} > 0, \; \frac{\partial e}{\partial i^*} > 0$$

in the short run, and

$$\frac{\partial y_1}{\partial i^*} = \frac{\partial y_2}{\partial i^*} = \frac{\partial y}{\partial i^*} < 0, \; \frac{\partial p_1}{\partial i^*} = \frac{\partial p_2}{\partial i^*} = \frac{\partial p}{\partial i^*} > 0, \; \frac{\partial e}{\partial i^*} > 0$$

in the long run.

3.2 Graphical Analysis

Next, we present a graphical analysis of the effects derived from the different shocks considered. Our graphical apparatus will consist of:

1. The *YY* and *LL* curves, linking the output levels of countries 1 and 2;
2. The aggregate demand functions of countries 1 and 2 AD_1 and AD_2, to be derived below; and
3. The short-run aggregate supply functions of countries 1 and 2 AS_1 and AS_2, that is, Eqs. 14 and 15.

We first derive the *YY* and *LL* curves.[5] Subtraction of (12) from (11), i.e., the equilibrium condition in the goods market of country 2 from the analogous equation for country 1, gives the *YY* curve:

$$y_1 = y_2 - \frac{3\beta}{1+2\gamma}(p_1 - p_2) + \frac{1}{1+2\gamma}(f_1 - f_2)$$

as a positively signed relationship between the output levels of countries 1 and 2. This is because an increase (decrease) in country 2s output would lead to a worsening (improvement) in its trade balance, which, to maintain equilibrium, would require a depreciation (appreciation) of the exchange rate, leading, in turn, to an increase (decrease) in country 1s output. The slope of the curve would be equal to one, given our assumption of identical economic frameworks for both countries.

In turn, from (13), i.e., the equilibrium condition in the union's money market, we get the *LL* curve:

$$y_1 = -y_2 - \frac{1}{\delta}(p_1 + p_2) + \frac{2}{\delta}m + \frac{2\varepsilon}{\delta}i^*$$

as a negatively-signed relationship between the output levels of countries 1 and 2. This is because an increase (decrease) in country 2s output would lead to an increase (decrease) in its demand for money, which, to maintain equilibrium, would require a decrease (increase) in country 1s demand for money, and hence a decrease (increase) in its output. The slope of the curve would be also equal to one, but now in absolute value.

Equations 11, 12 and 13 give the aggregate demand functions for countries 1 and 2, i.e., AD_1 and AD_2:

$$y_1 = -\frac{1}{2}\frac{1+2\gamma+3\beta\delta}{\delta(1+2\gamma)}p_1 - \frac{1}{2}\frac{1+2\gamma-3\beta\delta}{\delta(1+2\gamma)}p_2 + \frac{1}{\delta}m + \frac{1}{2}\frac{1}{1+2\gamma}(f_1 - f_2) + \frac{\varepsilon}{\delta}i^* \tag{19}$$

[5] These curves were first used by Levin (1983).

$$y_2 = -\frac{1}{2}\frac{1+2\gamma+3\beta\delta}{\delta(1+2\gamma)}p_2 - \frac{1}{2}\frac{1+2\gamma-3\beta\delta}{\delta(1+2\gamma)}p_1 + \frac{1}{\delta}m + \frac{1}{2}\frac{1}{1+2\gamma}(f_2-f_1) + \frac{\varepsilon}{\delta}i^* \tag{20}$$

Finally, we modify the *YY* and *LL* curves above, in order to remove p_1 and p_2. Thus, we obtain our modified *YY* curve after replacing $p_1 - p_2$ from (14) and (15):

$$y_1 = y_2 - \frac{3\beta(\sigma-\sigma')}{1+2\gamma+3\beta\phi}(p_{1,-1} - p_{2,-1}) + \frac{1}{1+2\gamma+3\beta\phi}(f_1-f_2) - \frac{3\beta\phi}{1+2\gamma+3\beta\phi}(s_1-s_2) \tag{21}$$

and, analogously, we obtain our modified *LL* curve after replacing $p_1 + p_2$ from (14) and (15):

$$y_1 = -y_2 - \frac{\sigma+\sigma'}{\delta+\phi}(p_{1,-1}+p_{2,-1}) - \frac{2(1-\sigma-\sigma')}{\delta+\phi}(p^*_{-1}+e_{-1}) + \frac{2}{\delta+\phi}m - \frac{\phi}{\delta+\phi}(s_1+s_2) + \frac{2\varepsilon}{\delta+\phi}i^* \tag{22}$$

Figure 1 shows the graphical apparatus used to discuss the shock effects in our model. The modified *YY* and *LL* curves [Eqs. 21 and 22] are depicted in panel (a) of the figure, and the aggregate demand and aggregate supply functions AD_1 and AS_1 for country 1 [Eqs. 19 and 14], and AD_2 and AS_2 for country 2 [Eqs. 20 and 15], appear in panels (b) and (c), respectively. Finally, panel (d) is used to connect panels (a) and (c). In the rest of this section, we examine the effects of different shocks on the monetary union, using the graphical apparatus shown in Fig. 1. As a general rule, point 1 in the figures denotes the pre-shock equilibrium, while points 2 and 3 denote, respectively, the short-run or transitory post-shock equilibrium, and the long-run or final equilibrium following the impact of the full set of shock effects (due to the assumed supply-side lags in the adjustment of prices).

We begin with the case of an (always common) expansionary monetary shock, $\Delta m > 0$, in Fig. 2. Starting from point 1, this shock means an aggregate demand expansion in the short run, both in countries 1 and 2 and the union as a whole. This demand expansion is due, not only to the shock itself, but also to the exchange rate depreciation; the *LL*, AD_1 and AD_2 curves shift to the right and countries 1 and 2 stay at point 2 in the figure. However, prices increase in both countries, which, together with the exchange rate depreciation, later cause *LL* to shift to the left (fully offsetting the initial shift to the right), and AS_1 and AS_2 also shift to the left due to the higher wage aspirations in both countries. In the end, countries 1 and 2 move to point 3 in Fig. 2, and, in the long run, the monetary shock is neutral for output, with a price increase equal to the exchange rate depreciation (leaving the real exchange rate unaltered). The result is the same in countries 1 and 2, and in the union as a whole.

The case of a specific expansionary expenditure shock in country 1, $\Delta f_1 > 0$, is depicted in Fig. 3; the case of a specific expansionary expenditure shock in

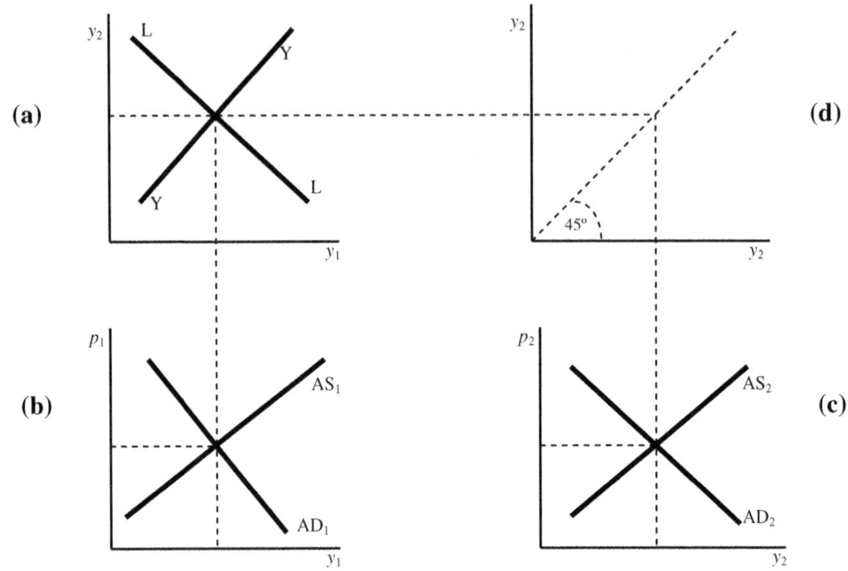

Fig. 1 Graphical representation of a monetary union

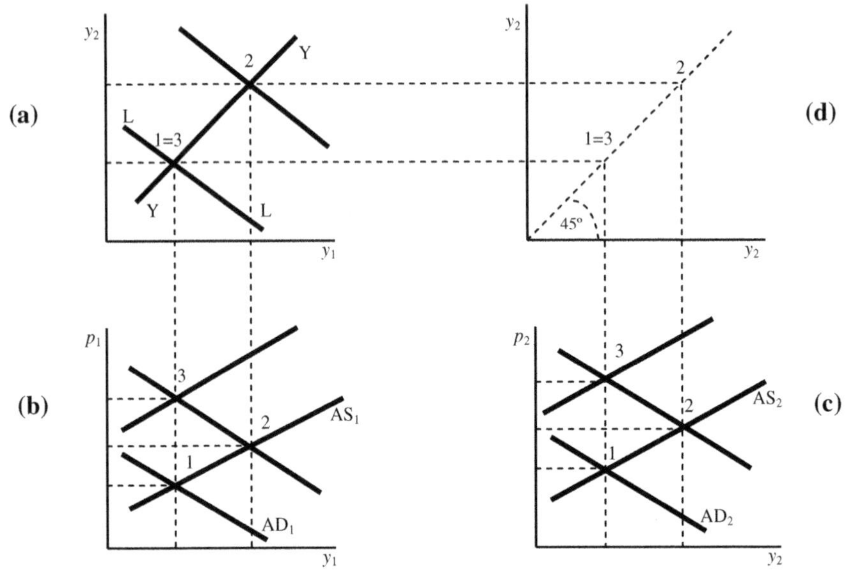

Fig. 2 Small monetary union. An expansionary monetary shock

country 2, $\Delta f_2 > 0$, is fully analogous, with the results for countries 1 and 2 interchanged. Aggregate demand expands in country 1 but contracts in country 2, due to the appreciation of the exchange rate, which, despite the positive

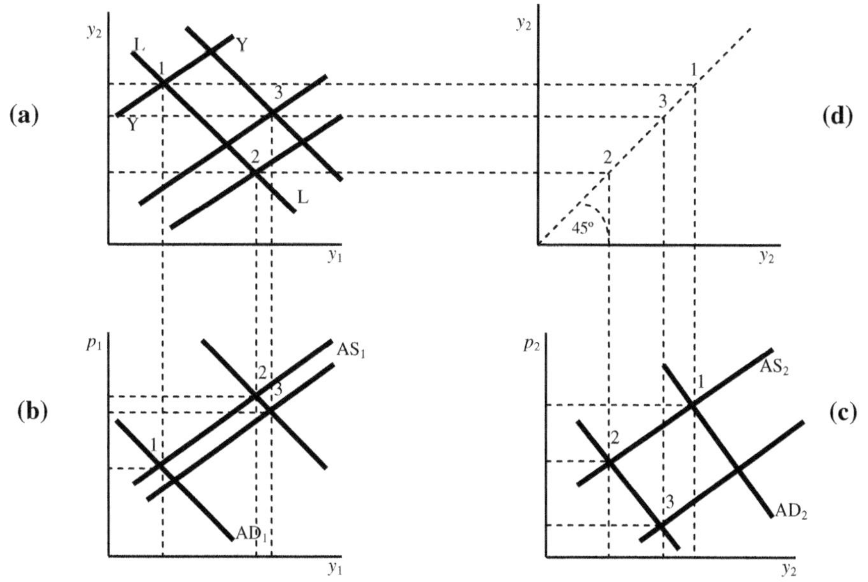

Fig. 3 Small monetary union. An expansionary expenditure shock specific to country 1

transmission of the shock through higher output in country 1, reduces output in country 2. In turn, the exchange rate appreciation and output contraction in country 2 partially offset the initial expansion in country 1. In terms of the figure, the *YY* and AD_1 curves shift to the right, and AD_2 to the left, so that countries 1 and 2 move from point 1 to point 2. Meanwhile, the effect on the union's output is nil since, due to our assumption of two symmetric countries, the demand expansion in country 1 fully offsets the demand contraction in country 2. Next, the exchange rate appreciation, through its effect on wage setting, causes *LL*, AS_1 and AS_2 to shift to the right, whereas the price increase in country 1 and the price decrease in country 2 shift *YY* to the left. Hence, countries 1 and 2 move to point 3 in Fig. 3.

The final result is an output increase with an ambiguous effect on prices in country 1, coupled with an ambiguous effect on output and a price decrease in country 2. The figure assumes a final output contraction in country 2. The effect on country 2s output depends on the relative weight of the real appreciation against the rest of the world, versus the output expansion in country 1 together with the real depreciation against the latter. Output increases in the union as a whole (so that the expansion in country 1 is greater than the potential contraction in country 2, when the shock is beggar-thy-neighbour, as in Fig. 3) and prices decrease (i.e., the price decrease in country 2 prevails despite any potential price increase in country 1).

We can derive the necessary conditions for a country-specific expenditure shock to be asymmetric, i.e., beggar-thy-neighbour in the other member country of the union; recall that such a condition must imply that $\frac{\partial y_2}{\partial f_1} = \frac{\partial y_1}{\partial f_2} < 0$. As can be seen

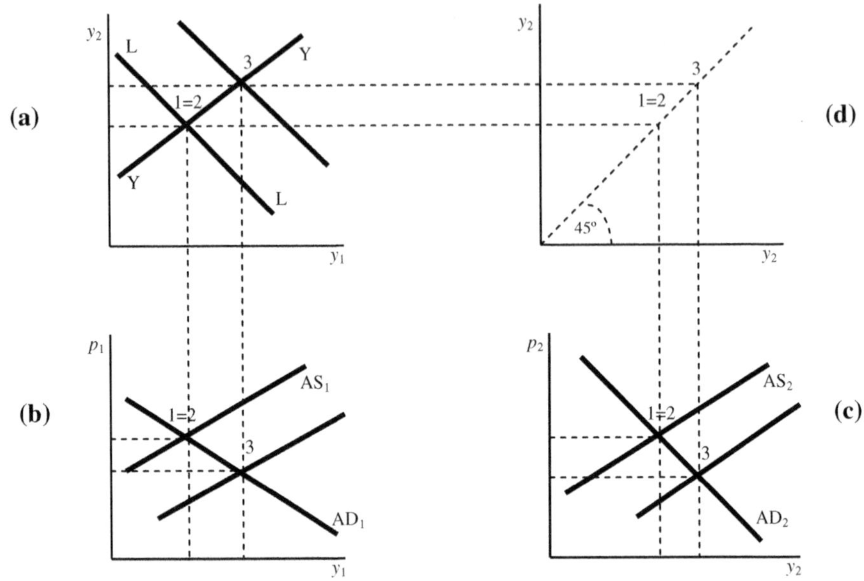

Fig. 4 Small monetary union. A common expansionary expenditure shock

from the multipliers in the Appendix, country-specific expenditure shocks are always asymmetric in the short run, whereas the condition for asymmetry in the long run, in terms of the degree of openness of the union, is that:

$$(1 - \sigma - \sigma') < \frac{\beta\phi(1 - \sigma + \sigma')}{3\beta\phi + 2\gamma(1 - \sigma + \sigma')}$$

where, if the partner country's share in the consumer price index is close to that of the country concerned (i.e., if $\sigma' \to \sigma$), the expression on the right-hand side becomes simply $\frac{\beta\phi}{3\beta\phi+2\gamma}$.

Notice that, as a general rule, the conditions under which a country-specific shock turns out to be asymmetric depend ultimately on the prevalence of the interest rate and the real exchange rate over aggregate demand, as the dominant shock transmission channel. More specifically, in the case of expenditure shocks, the probability of a country-specific expenditure shock being asymmetric in the long run for the other member of a monetary union increases with:

- a lower $(1 - \sigma - \sigma')$, i.e., the degree of openness of the union versus the rest of the world.
- a lower γ, i.e., the elasticity of domestic output with respect to foreign output.
- a higher β, i.e., the elasticity of output with respect to the real exchange rate.
- a higher ϕ, i.e., the elasticity of wages with respect to output.

A common, as opposed to country-specific, expansionary expenditure shock, $\Delta f_1 = \Delta f_2 = \Delta f > 0$, results in the situation depicted in Fig. 4. Since the aggregate

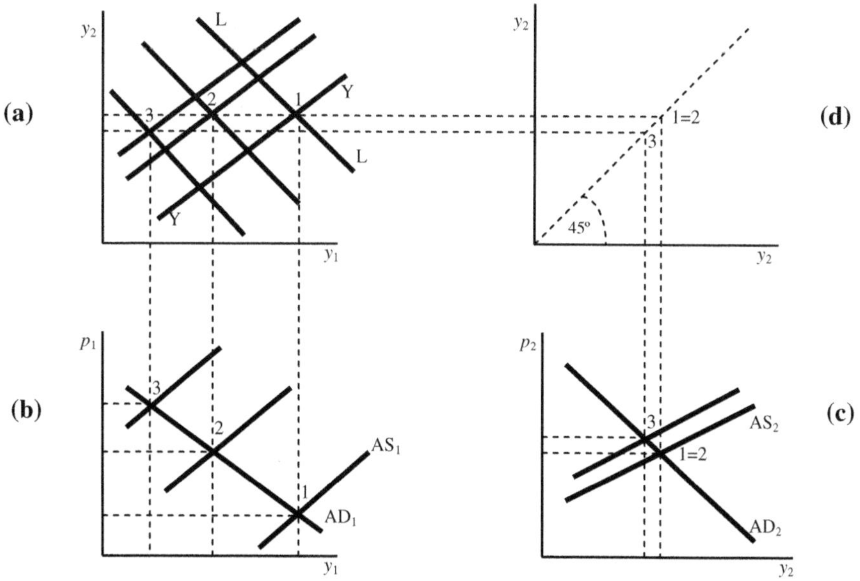

Fig. 5 Small monetary union. A contractionary supply shock specific to country 1

demand expansion is offset by the exchange rate appreciation, the short-run equilibrium at point 2 in the figure will coincide with the initial equilibrium at point 1. In graphical terms, the rightward shift of the *YY*, AD_1 and AD_2 curves due to the expansionary expenditure shock is fully offset by a leftward shift due to the exchange rate appreciation. As before, the appreciation of the exchange rate shifts *LL*, AS_1 and AS_2 to the right, so that countries 1 and 2 end up at point 3, with a long-run output expansion coupled with a price fall both for countries 1 and 2 and the union as a whole.

We now turn to the analysis of supply shocks, beginning with the case of a specific contractionary supply shock in country 1, $\Delta s_1 > 0$, as depicted in Fig. 5, which again is fully analogous with the case of a country-specific contractionary supply shock in country 2, $\Delta s_2 > 0$, with the results for the two countries interchanged. As output contracts and prices rise in country 1, the transmission of the shock to country 2 will be ambiguous, due to uncertainty about the consequences of the shock on the exchange rate. This is because lower output and higher prices in country 1 will lead to conflicting effects on the balance of payments, and hence on the exchange rate. Therefore, the effects of the shock on country 2 will be ambiguous, which means that the subsequent feedback effect on country 1 will also be ambiguous. Therefore, in Fig. 5, the *LL*, *YY* and AS_1 curves shift to the left, coinciding with an ambiguous shift in AD_2. For the sake of simplicity, we assume no short-run effect on country 2. However, despite this ambiguity regarding country 2, the union as a whole will experience the same effects as country 1, i.e., lower output and higher prices. In the long run, higher prices will shift *LL*, *YY*, AS_1

and AS_2 to the left, leading to an additional output fall and price increase in country 1 and the union as a whole, and (in this case) in country 2. In general, the long-run effects on country 2 are also ambiguous.

As in the case of expenditure shocks, we can derive the necessary conditions for a country-specific supply shock to be asymmetric, i.e., beggar-thy-neighbour in the other member country of the union. This now must imply that $\frac{\partial y_2}{\partial s_1} = \frac{\partial y_1}{\partial s_2} > 0$, so that, from the multipliers in the Appendix, the asymmetry conditions are:

$$1 + 2\gamma < 3\beta\delta$$

in the short run; and:

$$(1 - \sigma - \sigma') > \frac{(1 + 2\gamma)(1 - \sigma + \sigma')}{3}$$

in the long run, where, as before, if $\sigma' \to \sigma$, the expression on the right-hand side will become simply $\frac{1+2\gamma}{3}$.

Therefore, the probability of a country-specific supply shock being asymmetric in the short run increases with:

- a lower γ, i.e., the elasticity of domestic output with respect to foreign output.
- a higher β, i.e., the elasticity of output with respect to the real exchange rate.
- a higher δ, i.e., the elasticity of the demand for money with respect to output.

and the probability of a country-specific supply shock being asymmetric in the long run increases with:

- a higher $(1 - \sigma - \sigma')$, i.e., the degree of openness of the union versus the rest of the world.
- a lower γ, i.e., the elasticity of domestic output with respect to foreign output.

The case of a common contractionary supply shock, $\Delta s_1 = \Delta s_2 = \Delta s > 0$, is shown in Fig. 6. Now, output falls and prices rise unambiguously both in countries 1 and 2 and in the union, in the short and the long run; the effect on the exchange rate is again ambiguous. In terms of the figure, the *LL*, AS_1 and AS_2 curves shift to the left in the short run (with *YY* simultaneously experiencing a leftward and a rightward shift that fully offset each other), and the same shifts also occur in the long run following the rise in prices.

We conclude this section with a brief comment on external shocks. The effect of a positive shock to the trade balance following an increase in foreign output, $\Delta y^* > 0$, would be analogous to the case of a common expansionary expenditure shock as shown in Fig. 4. In turn, a positive shock to the trade balance following an increase in foreign prices, $\Delta p^* > 0$, would have no effect either in the short or the long run. The only effect would be an exchange rate appreciation equal, in absolute value, to the initial increase in foreign prices (simultaneous leftward and

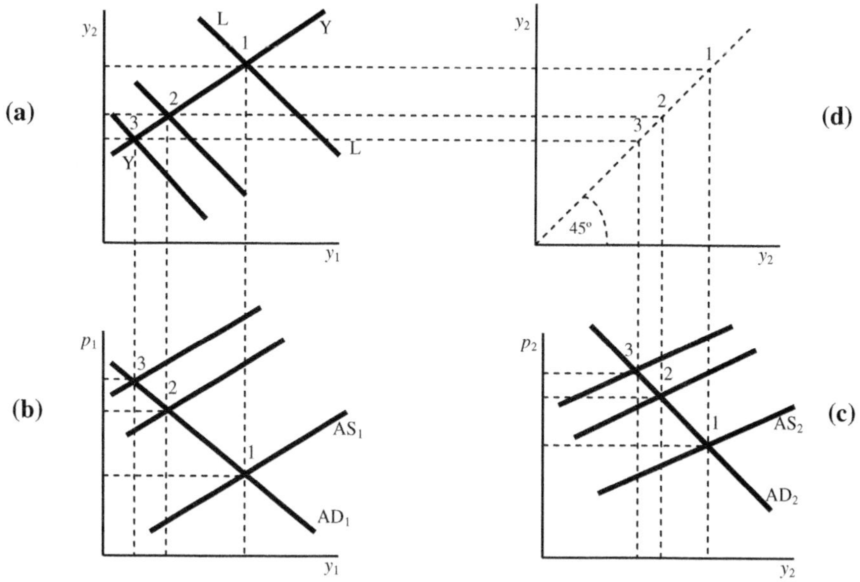

Fig. 6 Small monetary union. A common contractionary supply shock

rightward shifts in *LL*, AS_1 and AS_2 fully offsetting each other). Finally, the effect of a negative shock to capital flows following an increase in the foreign interest rate, $\Delta i^* > 0$, is analogous to the case of an expansionary monetary shock as shown in Fig. 2. The only difference is that the short-run effects are now quantitatively smaller, with an output fall in the long run, both in countries 1 and 2 and in the union as a whole (the initial rightward shift in *LL* is smaller than its later leftward shift due to the rise in prices and the exchange rate depreciation).

4 The Model for a Large Monetary Union

4.1 Shock Multipliers

The model for a large monetary union, shown in Table 2, comprises Eqs. 11–18, with eight endogenous variables: y_1, y_2, p_1, p_2, e, y^*, p^*, and i^*. As in the case of the small monetary union, we first show the short-run multipliers, obtained after solving the model given by Eqs. 11–18; and then the long-run multipliers, obtained from the solution of the long-run version of the model, i.e., that given by Eqs. 11–13, 14′, 15′, 16, 17, and 18′. A summary of the results is presented in Table 4.

Table 4 Effects of shocks: large monetary union

		Effects on: Output	Prices	Exchange rate	Rest of the world: Output	Rest of the world: Prices	Rest of the world: Interest rate
A. Common shocks ($d \neq 0$)							
Shocks		$\frac{\partial y_1}{\partial d} = \frac{\partial y_2}{\partial d} = \frac{\partial y}{\partial d}$	$\frac{\partial p_1}{\partial d} = \frac{\partial p_2}{\partial d} = \frac{\partial p}{\partial d}$	$\frac{\partial e}{\partial d}$	$\frac{\partial y^*}{\partial d}$	$\frac{\partial p^*}{\partial d}$	$\frac{\partial i^*}{\partial d}$
Monetary	sr	+	+	+	–	–	–
m	lr	0	1	1	0	0	0
Expenditure	sr	+	+	–	+	+	+
f	lr	+	±	–	–	+	+
Supply	sr = lr	–	+	±	+ (sr)	+	+
s					– (lr)		
Foreign monetary	sr	–	–	–	+	+	–
m^*	lr	0	0	–1	0	1	0
Foreign expenditure	sr	+	+	+	+	+	+
f^*	lr	–	+	+	+	±	+
Foreign supply	sr	+	+	±	–	+	+
s^*	lr	–	+	±	–	+	+

B. Country-specific shocks ($d_i \neq 0,\ d_j = 0$)		Output			Prices			Exchange rate	RoW Output	RoW Prices	RoW Interest rate
Shocks		$\frac{\partial y_1}{\partial d_1} = \frac{\partial y_2}{\partial d_2}$	$\frac{\partial y_2}{\partial d_1} = \frac{\partial y_1}{\partial d_2}$	$\frac{\partial y}{\partial d_1} = \frac{\partial y}{\partial d_2}$	$\frac{\partial p_1}{\partial d_1} = \frac{\partial p_2}{\partial d_2}$	$\frac{\partial p_2}{\partial d_1} = \frac{\partial p_1}{\partial d_2}$	$\frac{\partial p}{\partial d_1} = \frac{\partial p}{\partial d_2}$	$\frac{\partial e}{\partial d_1} = \frac{\partial e}{\partial d_2}$	$\frac{\partial y^*}{\partial d_1} = \frac{\partial y^*}{\partial d_2}$	$\frac{\partial p^*}{\partial d_1} = \frac{\partial p^*}{\partial d_2}$	$\frac{\partial i^*}{\partial d_1} = \frac{\partial i^*}{\partial d_2}$
Expenditure	sr	+	±	+	+	±	+	–	+	+	+
f_1, f_2	lr	+	±	+	±	±	±	–	–	+	+
Supply	sr = lr	–	±	–	+	±	+	±	+ (sr)	+	+
s_1, s_2									– (lr)		

Notes (i) sr = short run, lr = long run
(ii) $d = m, f, s, m^*, f^*, s^*$
(iii) $d_i, d_j = f_i, f_j, s_i, s_j$ $(i, j = 1, 2)$

The signs of the multipliers for the different shocks are now:

(A) Monetary shocks

$$\frac{\partial y_1}{\partial m} = \frac{\partial y_2}{\partial m} = \frac{\partial y}{\partial m} > 0, \ \frac{\partial p_1}{\partial m} = \frac{\partial p_2}{\partial m} = \frac{\partial p}{\partial m} > 0$$

$$\frac{\partial y^*}{\partial m} < 0, \ \frac{\partial p^*}{\partial m} < 0$$

$$\frac{\partial e}{\partial m} > 0, \quad \frac{\partial i^*}{\partial m} < 0$$

in the short run, and

$$\frac{\partial y_1}{\partial m} = \frac{\partial y_2}{\partial m} = \frac{\partial y}{\partial m} = 0, \ \frac{\partial p_1}{\partial m} = \frac{\partial p_2}{\partial m} = \frac{\partial p}{\partial m} = 1$$

$$\frac{\partial y^*}{\partial m} = 0, \ \frac{\partial p^*}{\partial m} = 0$$

$$\frac{\partial e}{\partial m} = 1, \quad \frac{\partial i^*}{\partial m} = 0$$

in the long run.

(B) Expenditure shocks

(B.1) Country-specific expenditure shocks

$$\frac{\partial y_1}{\partial f_1} = \frac{\partial y_2}{\partial f_2} > 0, \ \frac{\partial y_2}{\partial f_1} = \frac{\partial y_1}{\partial f_2} \lesseqgtr 0, \ \frac{\partial y}{\partial f_1} = \frac{\partial y}{\partial f_2} > 0$$

$$\frac{\partial p_1}{\partial f_1} = \frac{\partial p_2}{\partial f_2} > 0, \ \frac{\partial p_2}{\partial f_1} = \frac{\partial p_1}{\partial f_2} \lesseqgtr 0, \ \frac{\partial p}{\partial f_1} = \frac{\partial p}{\partial f_2} > 0$$

$$\frac{\partial y^*}{\partial f_1} = \frac{\partial y^*}{\partial f_2} > 0, \quad \frac{\partial p^*}{\partial f_1} = \frac{\partial p^*}{\partial f_2} > 0$$

$$\frac{\partial e}{\partial f_1} = \frac{\partial e}{\partial f_2} < 0, \quad \frac{\partial i^*}{\partial f_1} = \frac{\partial i^*}{\partial f_2} > 0$$

in the short run, and

$$\frac{\partial y_1}{\partial f_1} = \frac{\partial y_2}{\partial f_2} > 0, \ \frac{\partial y_2}{\partial f_1} = \frac{\partial y_1}{\partial f_2} \lesseqgtr 0, \ \frac{\partial y}{\partial f_1} = \frac{\partial y}{\partial f_2} > 0$$

$$\frac{\partial p_1}{\partial f_1} = \frac{\partial p_2}{\partial f_2} \lesseqgtr 0, \ \frac{\partial p_2}{\partial f_1} = \frac{\partial p_1}{\partial f_2} \lesseqgtr 0, \ \frac{\partial p}{\partial f_1} = \frac{\partial p}{\partial f_2} \lesseqgtr 0$$

$$\frac{\partial y^*}{\partial f_1} = \frac{\partial y^*}{\partial f_2} < 0, \quad \frac{\partial p^*}{\partial f_1} = \frac{\partial p^*}{\partial f_2} > 0$$

$$\frac{\partial e}{\partial f_1} = \frac{\partial e}{\partial f_2} < 0, \quad \frac{\partial i^*}{\partial f_1} = \frac{\partial i^*}{\partial f_2} > 0$$

in the long run.

(B.2) Common expenditure shocks

$$\frac{\partial y_1}{\partial f} = \frac{\partial y_2}{\partial f} = \frac{\partial y}{\partial f} > 0, \quad \frac{\partial p_1}{\partial f} = \frac{\partial p_2}{\partial f} = \frac{\partial p}{\partial f} > 0$$

$$\frac{\partial y^*}{\partial f} > 0, \quad \frac{\partial p^*}{\partial f} > 0$$

$$\frac{\partial e}{\partial f} < 0, \quad \frac{\partial i^*}{\partial f} > 0$$

in the short run, and

$$\frac{\partial y_1}{\partial f} = \frac{\partial y_2}{\partial f} = \frac{\partial y}{\partial f} > 0, \quad \frac{\partial p_1}{\partial f} = \frac{\partial p_2}{\partial f} = \frac{\partial p}{\partial f} \lesseqgtr 0$$

$$\frac{\partial y^*}{\partial f} < 0, \quad \frac{\partial p^*}{\partial f} > 0$$

$$\frac{\partial e}{\partial f} < 0, \quad \frac{\partial i^*}{\partial f} > 0$$

in the long run.

(C) Supply shocks

(C.1) Country-specific supply shocks

$$\frac{\partial y_1}{\partial s_1} = \frac{\partial y_2}{\partial s_2} < 0, \quad \frac{\partial y_2}{\partial s_1} = \frac{\partial y_1}{\partial s_2} \lesseqgtr 0, \quad \frac{\partial y}{\partial s_1} = \frac{\partial y}{\partial s_2} < 0$$

$$\frac{\partial p_1}{\partial s_1} = \frac{\partial p_2}{\partial s_2} > 0, \quad \frac{\partial p_2}{\partial s_1} = \frac{\partial p_1}{\partial s_2} \lesseqgtr 0, \quad \frac{\partial p}{\partial s_1} = \frac{\partial p}{\partial s_2} > 0$$

$$\frac{\partial y^*}{\partial s_1} = \frac{\partial y^*}{\partial s_2} > 0 \text{ (short run)}, \quad \frac{\partial y^*}{\partial s_1} = \frac{\partial y^*}{\partial s_2} < 0 \text{ (long run)}, \quad \frac{\partial p^*}{\partial s_1} = \frac{\partial p^*}{\partial s_2} > 0$$

$$\frac{\partial e}{\partial s_1} = \frac{\partial e}{\partial s_2} \lesseqgtr 0, \quad \frac{\partial i^*}{\partial s_1} = \frac{\partial i^*}{\partial s_2} > 0$$

both in the short run and in the long run (except for the case of y^*).

(C.2) Common supply shocks

$$\frac{\partial y_1}{\partial s} = \frac{\partial y_2}{\partial s} = \frac{\partial y}{\partial s} < 0, \quad \frac{\partial p_1}{\partial s} = \frac{\partial p_2}{\partial s} = \frac{\partial p}{\partial s} > 0$$

$$\frac{\partial y^*}{\partial s} > 0 \text{ (short run)}, \quad \frac{\partial y^*}{\partial s} < 0 \text{ (long run)}, \quad \frac{\partial p^*}{\partial s} > 0$$

$$\frac{\partial e}{\partial s} \lesseqgtr 0, \quad \frac{\partial i^*}{\partial s} > 0$$

both in the short run and in the long run (except for the case of y^*).

(D) External shocks

(D.1) Foreign monetary shocks

$$\frac{\partial y_1}{\partial m^*} = \frac{\partial y_2}{\partial m^*} = \frac{\partial y}{\partial m^*} < 0, \quad \frac{\partial p_1}{\partial m^*} = \frac{\partial p_2}{\partial m^*} = \frac{\partial p}{\partial m^*} < 0$$

$$\frac{\partial y^*}{\partial m^*} > 0, \quad \frac{\partial p^*}{\partial m^*} > 0$$

$$\frac{\partial e}{\partial m^*} < 0, \quad \frac{\partial i^*}{\partial m^*} < 0$$

in the short run, and

$$\frac{\partial y_1}{\partial m^*} = \frac{\partial y_2}{\partial m^*} = \frac{\partial y}{\partial m^*} = \frac{\partial p_1}{\partial m^*} = \frac{\partial p_2}{\partial m^*} = \frac{\partial p}{\partial m^*} = 0$$

$$\frac{\partial y^*}{\partial m^*} = 0, \quad \frac{\partial p^*}{\partial m^*} = 1$$

$$\frac{\partial e}{\partial m^*} = -1, \quad \frac{\partial i^*}{\partial m^*} = 0$$

in the long run.

(D.2) Foreign expenditure shocks

$$\frac{\partial y_1}{\partial f^*} = \frac{\partial y_2}{\partial f^*} = \frac{\partial y}{\partial f^*} > 0, \quad \frac{\partial p_1}{\partial f^*} = \frac{\partial p_2}{\partial f^*} = \frac{\partial p}{\partial f^*} > 0$$

$$\frac{\partial y^*}{\partial f^*} > 0, \quad \frac{\partial p^*}{\partial f^*} > 0$$

$$\frac{\partial e}{\partial f^*} > 0, \quad \frac{\partial i^*}{\partial f^*} > 0$$

in the short run, and

$$\frac{\partial y_1}{\partial f^*} = \frac{\partial y_2}{\partial f^*} = \frac{\partial y}{\partial f^*} < 0, \quad \frac{\partial p_1}{\partial f^*} = \frac{\partial p_2}{\partial f^*} = \frac{\partial p}{\partial f^*} > 0$$

$$\frac{\partial y^*}{\partial f^*} > 0, \quad \frac{\partial p^*}{\partial f^*} \lesseqgtr 0$$

$$\frac{\partial e}{\partial f^*} > 0, \quad \frac{\partial i^*}{\partial f^*} > 0$$

in the long run.

(D.3) Foreign supply shocks

$$\frac{\partial y_1}{\partial s^*} = \frac{\partial y_2}{\partial s^*} = \frac{\partial y}{\partial s^*} > 0, \quad \frac{\partial p_1}{\partial s^*} = \frac{\partial p_2}{\partial s^*} = \frac{\partial p}{\partial s^*} > 0$$

$$\frac{\partial y^*}{\partial s^*} < 0, \quad \frac{\partial p^*}{\partial s^*} > 0$$

$$\frac{\partial e}{\partial s^*} \lesseqgtr 0, \quad \frac{\partial i^*}{\partial s^*} > 0$$

in the short run, and

$$\frac{\partial y_1}{\partial s^*} = \frac{\partial y_2}{\partial s^*} = \frac{\partial y}{\partial s^*} < 0, \quad \frac{\partial p_1}{\partial s^*} = \frac{\partial p_2}{\partial s^*} = \frac{\partial p}{\partial s^*} > 0$$

$$\frac{\partial y^*}{\partial s^*} < 0, \quad \frac{\partial p^*}{\partial s^*} > 0$$

$$\frac{\partial e}{\partial s^*} \lesseqgtr 0, \quad \frac{\partial i^*}{\partial s^*} > 0$$

in the long run.

4.2 Graphical Analysis

The graphical representation of the model for the large monetary union is analogous to that of the small monetary union. The short-run aggregate supply functions AS_1 and AS_2, Eqs. 14 and 15, will be used as before. Notice, with respect to the aggregate demand functions AD_1 and AD_2, that Eqs. 19 and 20 above include i^*, which is now an endogenous variable. We proceed by first adding together: (1) the goods market equilibrium conditions for the union and the rest of the world (i.e., Eqs. 1, after replacing 3, and 16); and (2) the money market equilibrium conditions for the union and the rest of the world (i.e., Eqs. 2, after replacing 3, and 17). The solution of the two-equation system for i^*, after some rearrangement, gives:

$$i^* = \frac{1}{2}\frac{(1-\gamma)}{\alpha\delta + \varepsilon(1-\gamma)}(p+p^*) - \frac{1}{2}\frac{(1-\gamma)}{\alpha\delta + \varepsilon(1-\gamma)}(m+m^*) + \frac{1}{2}\frac{\delta}{\alpha\delta + \varepsilon(1-\gamma)}(f+f^*)$$

Now, by replacing this expression for i^* in Eqs. 19 and 20, we obtain the aggregate demand functions AD_1 and AD_2 for the large monetary union:

$$\begin{aligned} y_1 = &-\frac{1}{4}\frac{(1+2\gamma)(2\alpha\delta+\varepsilon(1-\gamma))+6\beta\delta(\alpha\delta+\varepsilon(1-\gamma))}{(1+2\gamma)\delta(\alpha\delta+\varepsilon(1-\gamma))}p_1 \\ &-\frac{1}{4}\frac{(1+2\gamma)(2\alpha\delta+\varepsilon(1-\gamma))-6\beta\delta(\alpha\delta+\varepsilon(1-\gamma))}{(1+2\gamma)\delta(\alpha\delta+\varepsilon(1-\gamma))}p_2 \\ &+\frac{1}{2}\frac{\varepsilon(1-\gamma)}{\delta(\alpha\delta+\varepsilon(1-\gamma))}p^* + \frac{1}{2}\frac{2\alpha\delta+\varepsilon(1-\gamma)}{\delta(\alpha\delta+\varepsilon(1-\gamma))}m + \frac{1}{4}\frac{\varepsilon(1+2\gamma)+2(\alpha\delta+\varepsilon(1-\gamma))}{(1+2\gamma)(\alpha\delta+\varepsilon(1-\gamma))}f_1 \\ &+\frac{1}{4}\frac{\varepsilon(1+2\gamma)-2(\alpha\delta+\varepsilon(1-\gamma))}{(1+2\gamma)(\alpha\delta+\varepsilon(1-\gamma))}f_2 - \frac{1}{2}\frac{\varepsilon(1-\gamma)}{\delta(\alpha\delta+\varepsilon(1-\gamma))}m^* + \frac{1}{2}\frac{\varepsilon}{\alpha\delta+\varepsilon(1-\gamma)}f^* \end{aligned} \tag{23}$$

and

$$\begin{aligned} y_2 = &-\frac{1}{4}\frac{(1+2\gamma)(2\alpha\delta+\varepsilon(1-\gamma))+6\beta\delta(\alpha\delta+\varepsilon(1-\gamma))}{(1+2\gamma)\delta(\alpha\delta+\varepsilon(1-\gamma))}p_2 \\ &-\frac{1}{4}\frac{(1+2\gamma)(2\alpha\delta+\varepsilon(1-\gamma))-6\beta\delta(\alpha\delta+\varepsilon(1-\gamma))}{(1+2\gamma)\delta(\alpha\delta+\varepsilon(1-\gamma))}p_1 \\ &+\frac{1}{2}\frac{\varepsilon(1-\gamma)}{\delta(\alpha\delta+\varepsilon(1-\gamma))}p^* + \frac{1}{2}\frac{2\alpha\delta+\varepsilon(1-\gamma)}{\delta(\alpha\delta+\varepsilon(1-\gamma))}m + \frac{1}{4}\frac{\varepsilon(1+2\gamma)-2(\alpha\delta+\varepsilon(1-\gamma))}{(1+2\gamma)(\alpha\delta+\varepsilon(1-\gamma))}f_1 \\ &+\frac{1}{4}\frac{\varepsilon(1+2\gamma)+2(\alpha\delta+\varepsilon(1-\gamma))}{(1+2\gamma)(\alpha\delta+\varepsilon(1-\gamma))}f_2 - \frac{1}{2}\frac{\varepsilon(1-\gamma)}{\delta(\alpha\delta+\varepsilon(1-\gamma))}m^* + \frac{1}{2}\frac{\varepsilon}{\alpha\delta+\varepsilon(1-\gamma)}f^* \end{aligned} \tag{24}$$

Meanwhile, the *YY* curve is given by Eq. 21, i.e., as in Sect. 3.2:

$$\begin{aligned} y_1 = y_2 &- \frac{3\beta(\sigma-\sigma')}{1+2\gamma+3\beta\phi}(p_{1,-1}-p_{2,-1}) + \frac{1}{1+2\gamma+3\beta\phi}(f_1-f_2) \\ &- \frac{3\beta\phi}{1+2\gamma+3\beta\phi}(s_1-s_2) \end{aligned} \tag{21}$$

Lastly, finding $p + p^*$ from the short-run aggregate supply functions for the union and the rest of the world, (10) and (18), and substituting in the above expression for i^*, we get:

$$i^* = \frac{1}{2}\frac{(1-\gamma)}{\alpha(\delta+\phi)+\varepsilon(1-\gamma)}(p_{-1}+p^*_{-1}) - \frac{1}{2}\frac{(1-\gamma)}{\alpha(\delta+\phi)+\varepsilon(1-\gamma)}(m+m^*)$$
$$+\frac{1}{2}\frac{\delta+\phi}{\alpha(\delta+\phi)+\varepsilon(1-\gamma)}(f+f^*) + \frac{1}{2}\frac{\phi(1-\gamma)}{\alpha(\delta+\phi)+\varepsilon(1-\gamma)}(s+s^*)$$

which, once replaced in Eq. 22, gives the expression for the *LL* curve to be used in this section:

$$y_1 = -y_2 - \frac{1}{2}\frac{1}{\delta+\phi}\frac{2(\sigma+\sigma')[\alpha(\delta+\phi)+\varepsilon(1-\gamma)]-\varepsilon(1-\gamma)}{\alpha(\delta+\phi)+\varepsilon(1-\gamma)}(p_{1,-1}+p_{2,-1})$$
$$-\frac{1}{\delta+\phi}\frac{2(1-\sigma-\sigma')[\alpha(\delta+\phi)+\varepsilon(1-\gamma)]-\varepsilon(1-\gamma)}{\alpha(\delta+\phi)+\varepsilon(1-\gamma)}p^*_{-1} - \frac{2(1-\sigma-\sigma')}{\delta+\phi}e_{-1}$$
$$+\frac{1}{\delta+\phi}\frac{2\alpha(\delta+\phi)+\varepsilon(1-\gamma)}{\alpha(\delta+\phi)+\varepsilon(1-\gamma)}m + \frac{1}{2}\frac{\varepsilon}{\alpha(\delta+\phi)+\varepsilon(1-\gamma)}(f_1+f_2)$$
$$-\frac{1}{2}\frac{\phi}{\delta+\phi}\frac{2\alpha(\delta+\phi)+\varepsilon(1-\gamma)}{\alpha(\delta+\phi)+\varepsilon(1-\gamma)}(s_1+s_2) - \frac{1}{\delta+\phi}\frac{\varepsilon(1-\gamma)}{\alpha(\delta+\phi)+\varepsilon(1-\gamma)}m^*$$
$$+\frac{\varepsilon}{\alpha(\delta+\phi)+\varepsilon(1-\gamma)}f^* + \frac{\phi}{\delta+\phi}\frac{\varepsilon(1-\gamma)}{\alpha(\delta+\phi)+\varepsilon(1-\gamma)}s^* \quad (25)$$

We can now examine the effects of the different shocks using our graphical representation. Beginning again with the case of an expansionary monetary shock within the union, $\Delta m > 0$, the effects of this shock on the countries of the union are fairly analogous to those that emerge in the small monetary union; see Fig. 2 above. The only difference is that the depreciation of the exchange rate of the union now means an appreciation of the foreign exchange rate, leading to a demand contraction in the rest of the world, with falling output and prices. This, in turn, means less short-run expansion in the union, via lower external demand and a lower real exchange rate depreciation (in terms of Fig. 2, both AD_1 and AD_2 undergo a lower shift rightwards). In the long run, output in the union returns to its initial level, with prices rising by the same amount as the exchange rate depreciation; and the initial contraction in the rest of the world is exactly offset by the short-run demand expansion in the union. In other words, a monetary shock within the union would be beggar-thy-neighbour in the short run, and would have no effect on the rest of the world in the long run.

The case of a country-specific expansionary expenditure shock in country 1, $\Delta f_1 > 0$, is depicted in Fig. 7. The effects of a country-specific expansionary expenditure shock in country 2, $\Delta f_2 > 0$, would again be their mirror image. Although the results for country 1 are similar to those of the small monetary union case, the exchange rate appreciation now means a depreciation of the foreign exchange rate, leading to a demand expansion in the rest of the world. This increases foreign output and prices and causes an ambiguous effect on country 2s output, due to higher external demand and lower real exchange rate appreciation. Coupled with the increase in country 1s output, this will also produce an increase

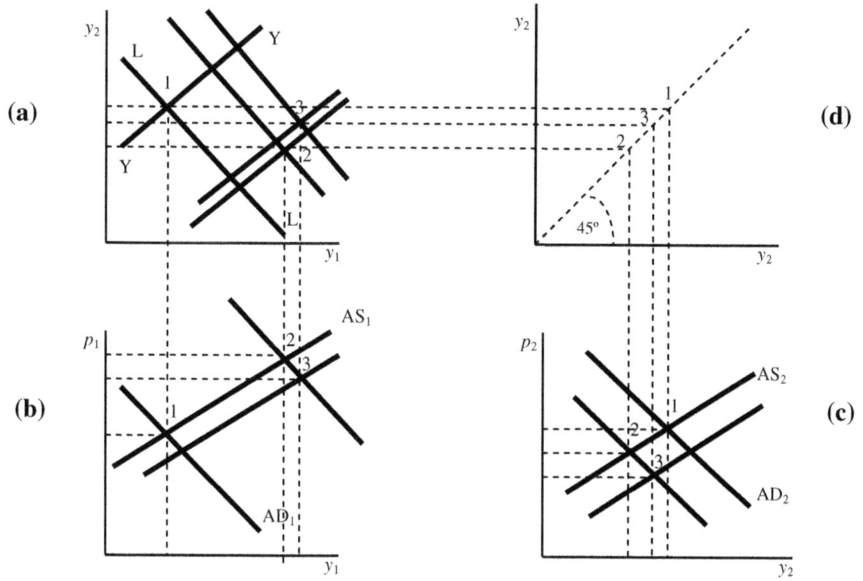

Fig. 7 Large monetary union. An expansionary expenditure shock specific to country 1

in the union's output. In terms of Fig. 7, the *YY*, *LL* and AD_1 curves shift to the right, and we assume a leftward shift in AD_2 (which implies that the shift in *LL* is less than that in *YY*), so that country 2s output falls and countries 1 and 2 move from point 1 to point 2.

The exchange rate depreciation in the rest of the world leads to a contraction of aggregate supply and a fall in foreign output, which reduces the long-run output increase both in country 1 and in the union. The effect on country 2s output is still ambiguous. In Fig. 7, *YY* shifts to the left and, assuming that the effect of the exchange rate appreciation prevails, *LL*, AS_1 and AS_2 shift to the right, so that countries 1 and 2 move to point 3. As can be seen, in this case, output and prices rise in country 1, and fall in country 2. However, if the effect of price changes prevails over that of the appreciation of the exchange rate, *LL*, AS_1 and AS_2 will shift to the left, so that country 1s output increases by less and its prices by more; whereas country 2s output decreases by more, and its prices decrease by less (or might even increase).

As in the case of the small monetary union, we can derive the necessary conditions for a country-specific expenditure shock to be asymmetric from the multipliers in the Appendix. In the short run, the conditions are:

$$\gamma < \frac{2\alpha(\delta + \phi) + \varepsilon(1 - 3\beta\phi)}{4\varepsilon}$$

so that the probability of a country-specific expenditure shock being asymmetric in the short run increases with:

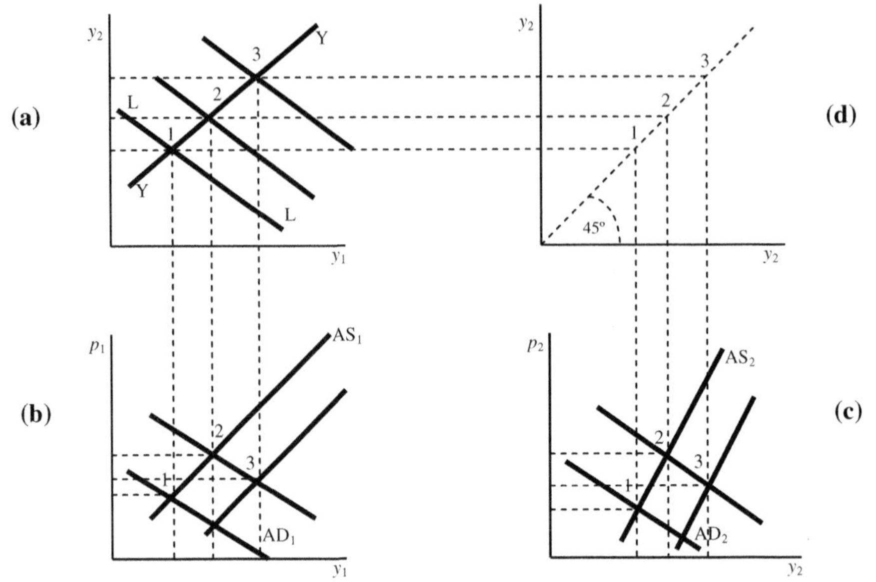

Fig. 8 Large monetary union. A common expansionary expenditure shock

- a lower γ, i.e., the elasticity of domestic output with respect to foreign output.
- a higher α, i.e., the elasticity of output with respect to the interest rate.
- a lower β, i.e., the elasticity of output with respect to the real exchange rate.
- a higher δ, i.e., the elasticity of the demand for money with respect to output.
- a lower ε, i.e., the elasticity of the demand for money with respect to the interest rate.while the condition for asymmetry in the long run is:

$$(1-\sigma-\sigma')<\frac{4\beta\phi\sigma'}{\beta\phi-(1-\sigma+\sigma')}$$

where, if $\sigma' \to \sigma$, the expression on the right-hand side becomes $\frac{4\beta\phi\sigma}{\beta\phi-1}$; and the probability of the shock being asymmetric[6] increases with:

- a lower $(1-\sigma-\sigma')$, i.e., the degree of openness of the union versus the rest of the world.
- a lower β, i.e., the elasticity of output with respect to the real exchange rate.

---

[6] Notice that the conditions for β and ϕ, are different from those derived for the case of the small monetary union (see above). The reason is that, in a large monetary union, an expansionary expenditure shock leads initially to an increase in both output and prices in the rest of the world, which tends to add to the expansionary effect within the union. Therefore, lower β and ϕ, mean smaller increases in both foreign output and prices (following, respectively, the depreciation of the exchange rate, and the rise in output that take place in the rest of the world).

- a lower ϕ,i.e., the elasticity of wages with respect to output.
- a higher σ', i.e., the partner country's share in the consumer price index.

Figure 8 shows the effects of a common expansionary expenditure shock, $\Delta f_1 = \Delta f_2 = \Delta f > 0$. As in the case of the country-specific shock, the exchange rate appreciation in the union means a depreciation of the foreign exchange rate, which leads to a demand expansion in the rest of the world, and hence also to a short-run demand expansion in the union. In Fig. 8, the LL, AD_1 and AD_2 curves shift to the right, countries 1 and 2 move from point 1 to point 2; and, again assuming that the effect of the exchange rate appreciation prevails, LL, AS_1 and AS_2 next shift to the right, so that countries 1 and 2 end up at point 3. As before, due to the final contraction in foreign output, the long-run output expansion in countries 1 and 2 and in the union is lower than in the small monetary union; and the effect on prices is ambiguous. The expansionary effect on output would be even lower if the effect of price changes had prevailed over that of the appreciation of the exchange rate, leading to a leftward shift in LL, AS_1 and AS_2.

Turning to their effects on the rest of the world, a (common or country-specific) expenditure shock within the union would be locomotive in the short run and beggar-thy-neighbour in the long run.

Meanwhile, the effects of supply shocks within the union would be fairly analogous to those analyzed in the case of the small monetary union, the conditions for a country-specific supply shock to be asymmetric being:

$$\frac{3\beta[2\alpha\delta(\delta+\phi)+(2\delta+\phi)\varepsilon(1-\gamma)]}{(1+2\gamma)[2\alpha(\delta+\phi)+\varepsilon(1-\gamma)]} > 1$$

in the short run; and:

$$(1-\sigma-\sigma') > \frac{\beta\phi[2(2+3\gamma)\sigma'+\gamma(1-\sigma+\sigma')]}{\beta\phi-(1+\gamma)(1+2\gamma)(1-\sigma+\sigma')}$$

in the long run, so that, if $\sigma' \to \sigma$, the expression on the right-hand side becomes $\frac{\beta\phi[2(2+3\gamma)\sigma+\gamma]}{\beta\phi-(1+\gamma)(1+2\gamma)}$. In particular, the probability of a country-specific supply shock being asymmetric in the long run increases with:

- a higher $(1-\sigma-\sigma')$, i.e., the degree of openness of the union versus the rest of the world.
- a higher β, i.e., the elasticity of output with respect to the real exchange rate.
- a higher ϕ,, i.e., the elasticity of wages with respect to output.
- a lower σ', i.e., the partner country's share in the consumer price index.

The effects of supply shocks on the rest of the world would be transmitted with the opposite sign in the short run, and with the same sign in the long run, i.e., they would be beggar-thy-neighbour in the short run and locomotive in the long run.

We conclude this section with an analysis of external shocks. An expansionary monetary shock in the rest of the world, $\Delta m^* > 0$, as shown in Fig. 9, leads to a foreign demand expansion together with an exchange rate depreciation in the rest of

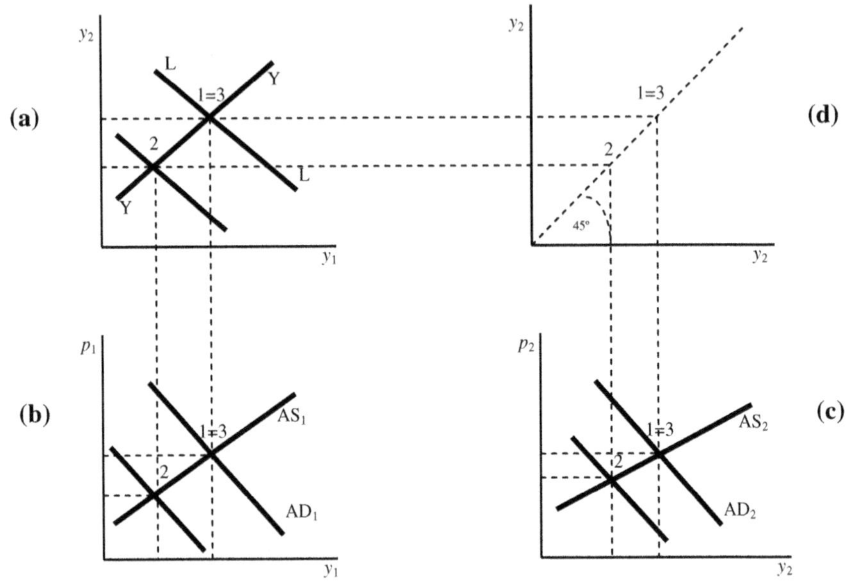

Fig. 9 Large monetary union. An expansionary monetary shock in the rest of the world

the world, i.e., an appreciation in the union, which contracts demand in the short run. Thus, the LL, AD_1 and AD_2 curves shift to the left in the figure, and countries 1 and 2 move from point 1 to point 2, with lower output and prices. Next, the short-run demand expansion in the rest of the world leads to a demand expansion in the union that fully offsets the previous contraction; while foreign output returns to its initial level and prices rise by the same amount as the foreign exchange rate depreciation. In Fig. 9 the LL, AD_1 and AD_2 curves return to their initial position, so that output and prices in countries 1 and 2 and in the union remain unchanged in the long run. Since prices in the union do not change, and the rise in foreign prices equals the appreciation of the exchange rate, the real exchange rate is unaffected, so AS_1 and AS_2 do not shift. Notice that the effects of this shock in the long run are equivalent to those of an increase in foreign prices in the small monetary union case.

Figure 10 illustrates the case of an expansionary expenditure shock in the rest of the world, $\Delta f^* > 0$. This shock means a foreign demand expansion coupled with an exchange rate appreciation in the rest of the world, i.e., a depreciation in the union. Demand expands in the union, leading to higher output and prices in the short run; the LL, AD_1 and AD_2 curves shift to the right, and countries 1 and 2 move from point 1 to point 2. Next, the combination of higher prices in the union and in the rest of the world, together with the exchange rate depreciation, contracts aggregate supply in the union and expands it in the rest of the world. Output falls and prices rise in the union, while output rises in the rest of the world, and the effect on prices is ambiguous. In Fig. 9, LL, AS_1 and AS_2 shift to the left and countries 1 and 2 end up at point 3. Notice that the effects of this shock are

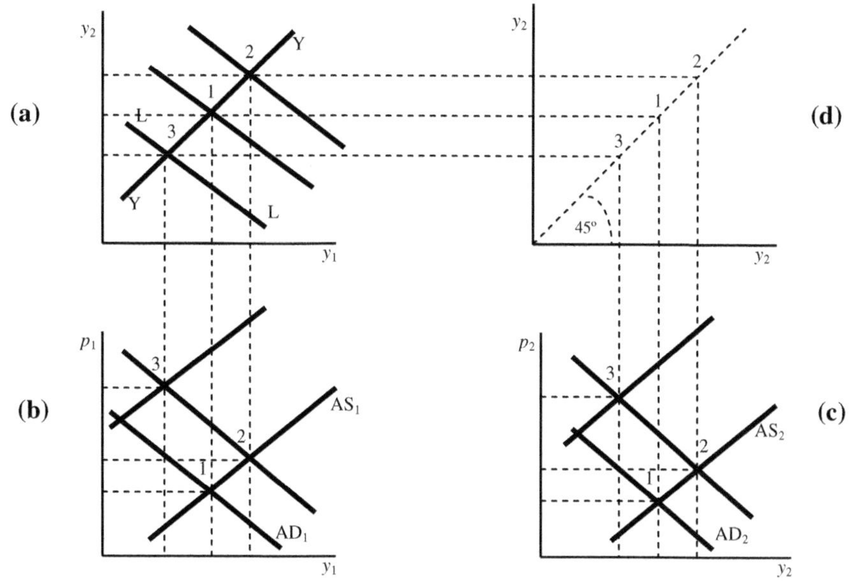

Fig. 10 Large monetary union. An expansionary expenditure shock in the rest of the world

equivalent to those of an increase in the foreign interest rate, as examined for a small monetary union.

Finally, the effects of a contractionary supply shock in the rest of the world, $\Delta s^* > 0$, are analogous to those of an expansionary expenditure shock in the rest of the world, and hence follow from Fig. 10.

5 Conclusions

We have developed a general framework for the macroeconomic modelling of monetary unions, which could be useful for policy analysis and teaching. The interest in modelling monetary unions is justified on the grounds that they have been suggested as an alternative to a system of fixed exchange rates, given the fragility of the latter in a world of very high capital mobility, as illustrated by the recent move towards EMU. Our ultimate aim was to "close" the M–F model, by completing the basic model to analyze a phenomenon of ever-increasing relevance.

Our framework of reference is the standard two-country M–F model with perfect capital mobility, extended to include the supply side in a context of rigid real wages. This model is modified so that the money market becomes common to two symmetric countries forming a monetary union, while maintaining a flexible exchange rate against the rest of the world. Two versions of the basic model, one for a small monetary union, the other for a large one, are presented, i.e., assuming the rest of the world's variables to be exogenous or endogenous, respectively. The model is solved for both the short and the long run, i.e., before and after prices fully adjust to equilibrium, respectively. The solutions to the models are presented for the different shocks analyzed (monetary, expenditure, supply, and external), both algebraically and graphically. The complete sets of equations for each model are shown in Tables 1 and 2, and a summary of their solutions in Tables 3 and 4, for the small and large monetary union, respectively.

A crucial point concerns the role of asymmetric shocks. The main feature of a monetary union is that all the member countries share a common monetary policy. It is clear, however, that a common monetary policy is of little use in coping with asymmetric shocks, i.e., those requiring a different policy response within each country concerned. Thus, the prevalence of asymmetric shocks is an impediment to the proper working of a monetary union. We have identified asymmetric shocks as those that are country-specific (i.e., they affect one country in the union, but not the other) and are transmitted to the other country with the opposite sign (i.e., they are of the "beggar-thy-neighbour" type). In addition, in deriving the conditions under which a particular shock becomes asymmetric, we find them to be ultimately dependent on the prevalence of the interest rate and the real exchange rate, over aggregate demand, as the dominant shock transmission channel.

Recall, furthermore, that, in order to simplify the analysis, we assumed a monetary union made up of two identical countries, where each country represents half of the union as a whole. Our framework, however, can be extended, without loss of generality, to the case of different-sized countries. Specifically, in relation to country-specific shocks, the smaller the country in which the shock originates, the less its effect on the union as a whole; and, if the share in the union of the country in question is less than one half, the shock will be asymmetric for the union as a whole.

The analysis described in this book could be extended in a number of ways. First, the model could be modified to incorporate a monetary policy rule, instead of a *LM* curve, following the now usual practice of many central banks. In addition, our basic framework could be used in policy coordination discussions, as shown in Díaz-Roldán (2005). Finally, the model could be empirically tested by calibrating particular values for the different coefficients, which might shed some light on the magnitude and sign of the effects, or identify the kind of shocks that would prevail in a specific monetary union, such as the EMU, for example.

References

Akerlof GA, Yellen JL (1985) Can small deviations from rationality make significant differences to economic equilibria? Am Econ Rev 75:708–720

Bajo-Rubio O (ed) (2003) Macroeconomic policy in an open economy: applications of the Mundell–Fleming model. Nova Science Publishers, New York

Ball L (2000) Near-rationality and inflation in two monetary regimes. Working paper 7988, National Bureau of Economic Research

Blanchard O (1997) Is there a core of usable macroeconomics? Am Econ Rev 87:244–246 Papers and Proceedings
Blanchard O (2009) Macroeconomics, 5th edn. Prentice Hall, Upper Saddle River
Carlberg M (2001) An economic analysis of monetary union. Springer, Berlin
Carlberg M (2003) Policy coordination in a monetary union. Springer, Berlin
Carlin W, Soskice D (2006) Macroeconomics: imperfections, institutions, and policies. Oxford University Press, Oxford
De Bonis V (1994) Stabilization policy in an exchange rate union: transmission, coordination and influence on the union cohesion. Physica-Verlag, Heidelberg
De Grauwe P (2009) Economics of monetary union, 8th edn. Oxford University Press, Oxford
Díaz-Roldán C (2005) La política económica en una unión monetaria: ¿Independencia o coordinación? Información Comercial Española 824:191–207
Dornbusch R (1980) Open economy macroeconomics. Basic Books, New York
Engel C (2000) Local-currency pricing and the choice of exchange-rate regime. Eur Econ Rev 44:1449–1472
Frenkel JA, Razin A (1987) The Mundell–Fleming model a quarter century later: a unified exposition. IMF Staff Pap 34:567–620
Krugman P (1995) What do we need to know about the international monetary system? In: Kenen PB (ed) Understanding Interdependence: The Macroeconomics of the Open Economy. Princeton University Press, Princeton, pp 509–529
Läufer NKA, Sundararajan S (1994) The international transmission of economic shocks in a three-country world under mixed exchange rates. J Int Money Finance 13:419–446
Layard R, Nickell S, Jackman R (1991) Unemployment: Macroeconomic performance and the labour market. Oxford University Press, Oxford
Levin JH (1983) A model of stabilisation policy in a jointly floating currency area. In: Bhandari JS, Putnam BH (eds) Economic Interdependence and Flexible Exchange Rates. The MIT Press, Cambridge, pp 329–349
Mankiw NG (2000) The inexorable and mysterious tradeoff between inflation and unemployment. Econ J 111:45–61
Mankiw NG (2010) Macroeconomics, 7th edn. Worth Publishers, New York
Marston RC (1984) Exchange rate unions as an alternative to flexible rates: the effects of real and monetary disturbances. In: Marston RC, Bilson JFO (eds) Exchange Rate Theory and Practice. The University of Chicago Press, Chicago, pp 407–442
Marston RC (1985) Stabilization policies in open economies. In: Jones RW, Kenen PB (eds) Handbook of International Economics, vol 2. North-Holland, Amsterdam, pp 859–916
Mundell RA (1961) A theory of optimum currency areas. Am Econ Rev 51:657–665
Mundell RA (1964) A reply: capital mobility and size. Can J Econ Polit Sci 30:421–431
Obstfeld M, Rogoff K (1995) The mirage of fixed exchange rates. J Econ Perspect 9:73–96
Rudd J, Whelan K (2006) Can rational expectations sticky-price models explain inflation dynamics? Am Econ Rev 96:303–320
Sachs J (1980) Wages, flexible exchange rates, and macroeconomic policy. Quart J Econ 94:731–747
Sargent TJ (1979) Macroeconomic theory. Academic Press, New York

Appendix: Solution of the Models

Small Monetary Union

Short Run

$$
\begin{aligned}
y_1 = {} & \frac{1}{\delta+\phi}m + \frac{1}{2}\frac{1}{1+2\gamma+3\beta\phi}f_1 - \frac{1}{2}\frac{1}{1+2\gamma+3\beta\phi}f_2 \\
& - \frac{1}{2}\frac{\phi[1+2\gamma+3\beta(\delta+2\phi)]}{(\delta+\phi)(1+2\gamma+3\beta\phi)}s_1 - \frac{1}{2}\frac{\phi(1+2\gamma-3\beta\delta)}{(\delta+\phi)(1+2\gamma+3\beta\phi)}s_2 + \frac{\varepsilon}{\delta+\phi}i^* \\
& - \frac{1}{2}\frac{\sigma[1+2\gamma+3\beta(\delta+2\phi)]+\sigma'(1+2\gamma-3\beta\delta)}{(\delta+\phi)(1+2\gamma+3\beta\phi)}p_{1,-1} \\
& - \frac{1}{2}\frac{\sigma(1+2\gamma-3\beta\delta)+\sigma'[1+2\gamma+3\beta(\delta+2\phi)]}{(\delta+\phi)(1+2\gamma+3\beta\phi)}p_{2,-1} - \frac{(1-\sigma-\sigma')}{\delta+\phi}p^*_{-1} \\
& - \frac{(1-\sigma-\sigma')}{\delta+\phi}e_{-1}
\end{aligned}
$$

$$
\begin{aligned}
y_2 = {} & \frac{1}{\delta+\phi}m - \frac{1}{2}\frac{1}{1+2\gamma+3\beta\phi}f_1 + \frac{1}{2}\frac{1}{1+2\gamma+3\beta\phi}f_2 \\
& - \frac{1}{2}\frac{\phi(1+2\gamma-3\beta\delta)}{(\delta+\phi)(1+2\gamma+3\beta\phi)}s_1 - \frac{1}{2}\frac{\phi[1+2\gamma+3\beta(\delta+2\phi)]}{(\delta+\phi)(1+2\gamma+3\beta\phi)}s_2 + \frac{\varepsilon}{\delta+\phi}i^* \\
& - \frac{1}{2}\frac{\sigma(1+2\gamma-3\beta\delta)+\sigma'[1+2\gamma+3\beta(\delta+2\phi)]}{(\delta+\phi)(1+2\gamma+3\beta\phi)}p_{1,-1} \\
& - \frac{1}{2}\frac{\sigma[1+2\gamma+3\beta(\delta+2\phi)]+\sigma'(1+2\gamma-3\beta\delta)}{(\delta+\phi)(1+2\gamma+3\beta\phi)}p_{2,-1} - \frac{(1-\sigma-\sigma')}{\delta+\phi}p^*_{-1} \\
& - \frac{(1-\sigma-\sigma')}{\delta+\phi}e_{-1}
\end{aligned}
$$

$$p_1 = \frac{\phi}{\delta+\phi}m + \frac{1}{2}\frac{\phi}{1+2\gamma+3\beta\phi}f_1 - \frac{1}{2}\frac{\phi}{1+2\gamma+3\beta\phi}f_2$$
$$+\frac{1}{2}\phi\frac{\phi(1+2\gamma+3\beta\delta)+2\delta(1+2\gamma)}{(\delta+\phi)(1+2\gamma+3\beta\phi)}s_1 - \frac{1}{2}\phi\frac{\phi(1+2\gamma-3\beta\delta)}{(\delta+\phi)(1+2\gamma+3\beta\phi)}s_2$$
$$+\frac{\varepsilon\phi}{\delta+\phi}i^* + \frac{1}{2}\frac{\sigma[\phi(1+2\gamma+3\beta\delta)+2\delta(1+2\gamma)]-\sigma'[\phi(1+2\gamma-3\beta\delta)]}{(\delta+\phi)(1+2\gamma+3\beta\phi)}p_{1,-1}$$
$$-\frac{1}{2}\frac{\sigma[\phi(1+2\gamma-3\beta\delta)]-\sigma'[\phi(1+2\gamma+3\beta\delta)+2\delta(1+2\gamma)]}{(\delta+\phi)(1+2\gamma+3\beta\phi)}p_{2,-1}$$
$$+\frac{\delta(1-\sigma-\sigma')}{\delta+\phi}p^*_{-1} + \frac{\delta(1-\sigma-\sigma')}{\delta+\phi}e_{-1}$$

$$p_2 = \frac{\phi}{\delta+\phi}m - \frac{1}{2}\frac{\phi}{1+2\gamma+3\beta\phi}f_1 + \frac{1}{2}\frac{\phi}{1+2\gamma+3\beta\phi}f_2$$
$$-\frac{1}{2}\phi\frac{\phi(1+2\gamma-3\beta\delta)}{(\delta+\phi)(1+2\gamma+3\beta\phi)}s_1 + \frac{1}{2}\phi\frac{\phi(1+2\gamma+3\beta\delta)+2\delta(1+2\gamma)}{(\delta+\phi)(1+2\gamma+3\beta\phi)}s_2$$
$$+\frac{\varepsilon\phi}{\delta+\phi}i^* - \frac{1}{2}\frac{\sigma[\phi(1+2\gamma-3\beta\delta)]-\sigma'[\phi(1+2\gamma+3\beta\delta)+2\delta(1+2\gamma)]}{(\delta+\phi)(1+2\gamma+3\beta\phi)}p_{1,-1}$$
$$+\frac{1}{2}\frac{\sigma[\phi(1+2\gamma+3\beta\delta)+2\delta(1+2\gamma)]-\sigma'[\phi(1+2\gamma-3\beta\delta)]}{(\delta+\phi)(1+2\gamma+3\beta\phi)}p_{2,-1}$$
$$+\frac{\delta(1-\sigma-\sigma')}{\delta+\phi}p^*_{-1} + \frac{\delta(1-\sigma-\sigma')}{\delta+\phi}e_{-1}$$

$$e = \frac{1+\beta\phi}{\beta(\delta+\phi)}m - \frac{1}{2\beta}f_1 - \frac{1}{2\beta}f_2 + \frac{1}{2}\frac{\phi(1-\beta\delta)}{\beta(\delta+\phi)}s_1 + \frac{1}{2}\frac{\phi(1-\beta\delta)}{\beta(\delta+\phi)}s_2 - \frac{\gamma}{\beta}y^* - p^*$$
$$+\frac{\alpha(\delta+\phi)+\varepsilon(1+\beta\phi)}{\beta(\delta+\phi)}i^* + \frac{1}{2}\frac{(1-\beta\delta)(\sigma+\sigma')}{\beta(\delta+\phi)}p_{1,-1} + \frac{1}{2}\frac{(1-\beta\delta)(\sigma+\sigma')}{\beta(\delta+\phi)}p_{2,-1}$$
$$+\frac{(1-\beta\delta)(1-\sigma-\sigma')}{\beta(\delta+\phi)}p^*_{-1} + \frac{(1-\beta\delta)(1-\sigma-\sigma')}{\beta(\delta+\phi)}e_{-1}$$

Long Run

$$
\begin{aligned}
y_1 = {} & \frac{1}{2}\frac{(1-\sigma-\sigma')[2(1+\gamma)(1-\sigma+\sigma')+3\beta\phi]+\beta\phi(1-\sigma+\sigma')}{[(1-\sigma-\sigma')+\beta\phi][(1+2\gamma)(1-\sigma+\sigma')+3\beta\phi]}f_1 \\
& + \frac{1}{2}\frac{(1-\sigma-\sigma')[2\gamma(1-\sigma+\sigma')+3\beta\phi]-\beta\phi(1-\sigma+\sigma')}{[(1-\sigma-\sigma')+\beta\phi][(1+2\gamma)(1-\sigma+\sigma')+3\beta\phi]}f_2 \\
& - \frac{1}{2}\frac{\beta\phi[3(1-\sigma-\sigma')+(1+2\gamma)(1-\sigma+\sigma')+6\beta\phi]}{[(1-\sigma-\sigma')+\beta\phi][(1+2\gamma)(1-\sigma+\sigma')+3\beta\phi]}s_1 \\
& - \frac{1}{2}\frac{\beta\phi[-3(1-\sigma-\sigma')+(1+2\gamma)(1-\sigma+\sigma')]}{[(1-\sigma-\sigma')+\beta\phi][(1+2\gamma)(1-\sigma+\sigma')+3\beta\phi]}s_2 \\
& + \frac{\gamma(1-\sigma-\sigma')}{(1-\sigma-\sigma')+\beta\phi}y^* - \frac{\alpha(1-\sigma-\sigma')}{(1-\sigma-\sigma')+\beta\phi}i^*
\end{aligned}
$$

$$
\begin{aligned}
y_2 = {} & \frac{1}{2}\frac{(1-\sigma-\sigma')[2\gamma(1-\sigma+\sigma')+3\beta\phi]-\beta\phi(1-\sigma+\sigma')}{[(1-\sigma-\sigma')+\beta\phi][(1+2\gamma)(1-\sigma+\sigma')+3\beta\phi]}f_1 \\
& + \frac{1}{2}\frac{(1-\sigma-\sigma')[2(1+\gamma)(1-\sigma+\sigma')+3\beta\phi]+\beta\phi(1-\sigma+\sigma')}{[(1-\sigma-\sigma')+\beta\phi][(1+2\gamma)(1-\sigma+\sigma')+3\beta\phi]}f_2 \\
& - \frac{1}{2}\frac{\beta\phi[-3(1-\sigma-\sigma')+(1+2\gamma)(1-\sigma+\sigma')]}{[(1-\sigma-\sigma')+\beta\phi][(1+2\gamma)(1-\sigma+\sigma')+3\beta\phi]}s_1 \\
& - \frac{1}{2}\frac{\beta\phi[3(1-\sigma-\sigma')+(1+2\gamma)(1-\sigma+\sigma')+6\beta\phi]}{[(1-\sigma-\sigma')+\beta\phi][(1+2\gamma)(1-\sigma+\sigma')+3\beta\phi]}s_2 \\
& + \frac{\gamma(1-\sigma-\sigma')}{(1-\sigma-\sigma')+\beta\phi}y^* - \frac{\alpha(1-\sigma-\sigma')}{(1-\sigma-\sigma')+\beta\phi}i^*
\end{aligned}
$$

$$
\begin{aligned}
p_1 = m & - \frac{1}{2}\frac{\delta(1-\sigma-\sigma')[(1+2\gamma)(1-\sigma+\sigma')+3\beta\phi]-\phi[(1-\sigma-\sigma')+\beta\phi]}{[(1-\sigma-\sigma')+\beta\phi][(1+2\gamma)(1-\sigma+\sigma')+3\beta\phi]}f_1 \\
& - \frac{1}{2}\frac{\delta(1-\sigma-\sigma')[(1+2\gamma)(1-\sigma+\sigma')+3\beta\phi]+\phi[(1-\sigma-\sigma')+\beta\phi]}{[(1-\sigma-\sigma')+\beta\phi][(1+2\gamma)(1-\sigma+\sigma')+3\beta\phi]}f_2 \\
& + \frac{1}{2}\phi\frac{\beta\delta[(1+2\gamma)(1-\sigma+\sigma')+3\beta\phi]+(1+2\gamma)[(1-\sigma-\sigma')+\beta\phi]}{[(1-\sigma-\sigma')+\beta\phi][(1+2\gamma)(1-\sigma+\sigma')+3\beta\phi]}s_1 \\
& + \frac{1}{2}\phi\frac{\beta\delta[(1+2\gamma)(1-\sigma+\sigma')+3\beta\phi]-(1+2\gamma)[(1-\sigma-\sigma')+\beta\phi]}{[(1-\sigma-\sigma')+\beta\phi][(1+2\gamma)(1-\sigma+\sigma')+3\beta\phi]}s_2 \\
& - \frac{\gamma\delta(1-\sigma-\sigma')}{(1-\sigma-\sigma')+\beta\phi}y^* + \frac{\alpha\delta(1-\sigma-\sigma')+\varepsilon[(1-\sigma-\sigma')+\beta\phi]}{(1-\sigma-\sigma')+\beta\phi}i^*
\end{aligned}
$$

$$
\begin{aligned}
p_2 = m &- \frac{1}{2}\frac{\delta(1-\sigma-\sigma')[(1+2\gamma)(1-\sigma+\sigma')+3\beta\phi]+\phi[(1-\sigma-\sigma')+\beta\phi]}{[(1-\sigma-\sigma')+\beta\phi][(1+2\gamma)(1-\sigma+\sigma')+3\beta\phi]}f_1 \\
&- \frac{1}{2}\frac{\delta(1-\sigma-\sigma')[(1+2\gamma)(1-\sigma+\sigma')+3\beta\phi]-\phi[(1-\sigma-\sigma')+\beta\phi]}{[(1-\sigma-\sigma')+\beta\phi][(1+2\gamma)(1-\sigma+\sigma')+3\beta\phi]}f_2 \\
&+ \frac{1}{2}\phi\frac{\beta\delta[(1+2\gamma)(1-\sigma+\sigma')+3\beta\phi]-(1+2\gamma)[(1-\sigma-\sigma')+\beta\phi]}{[(1-\sigma-\sigma')+\beta\phi][(1+2\gamma)(1-\sigma+\sigma')+3\beta\phi]}s_1 \\
&+ \frac{1}{2}\phi\frac{\beta\delta[(1+2\gamma)(1-\sigma+\sigma')+3\beta\phi]+(1+2\gamma)[(1-\sigma-\sigma')+\beta\phi]}{[(1-\sigma-\sigma')+\beta\phi][(1+2\gamma)(1-\sigma+\sigma')+3\beta\phi]}s_2 \\
&- \frac{\gamma\delta(1-\sigma-\sigma')}{(1-\sigma-\sigma')+\beta\phi}y^* + \frac{\alpha\delta(1-\sigma-\sigma')+\varepsilon[(1-\sigma-\sigma')+\beta\phi]}{(1-\sigma-\sigma')+\beta\phi}i^*
\end{aligned}
$$

$$
\begin{aligned}
e = m &- \frac{1}{2}\frac{\delta(1-\sigma-\sigma')+\phi}{(1-\sigma-\sigma')+\beta\phi}f_1 - \frac{1}{2}\frac{\delta(1-\sigma-\sigma')+\phi}{(1-\sigma-\sigma')+\beta\phi}f_2 - \frac{1}{2}\frac{(1-\beta\delta)\phi}{(1-\sigma-\sigma')+\beta\phi}s_1 \\
&- \frac{1}{2}\frac{(1-\beta\delta)\phi}{(1-\sigma-\sigma')+\beta\phi}s_2 - \frac{\gamma[\delta(1-\sigma-\sigma')+\phi]}{(1-\sigma-\sigma')+\beta\phi}y^* - p^* \\
&+ \frac{\alpha[\delta(1-\sigma-\sigma')+\phi]+\varepsilon[(1-\sigma-\sigma')+\beta\phi]}{(1-\sigma-\sigma')+\beta\phi}i^*
\end{aligned}
$$

Large Monetary Union

Short Run

$$
\begin{aligned}
y_1 = {} & \frac{1}{2}\frac{\varepsilon(1-\gamma)+2\alpha(\delta+\phi)}{(\delta+\phi)[\alpha(\delta+\phi)+\varepsilon(1-\gamma)]}m+\frac{1}{4}\frac{2\alpha(\delta+\phi)+3\varepsilon(1+\beta\phi)}{[\alpha(\delta+\phi)+\varepsilon(1-\gamma)](1+2\gamma+3\beta\phi)}f_1 \\
& -\frac{1}{4}\frac{2\alpha(\delta+\phi)+\varepsilon(1-4\gamma-3\beta\phi)}{[\alpha(\delta+\phi)+\varepsilon(1-\gamma)](1+2\gamma+3\beta\phi)}f_2 \\
& -\frac{1}{4}\phi\frac{6\beta\delta[\alpha\delta+\varepsilon(1-\gamma)]+\varepsilon[(1-\gamma)(1+2\gamma)]+2\alpha[(\delta+\phi)(1+2\gamma)]+9\beta\phi[2\alpha\delta+\varepsilon(1-\gamma)]+12\alpha\beta\phi^2}{(\delta+\phi)[\alpha(\delta+\phi)+\varepsilon(1-\gamma)](1+2\gamma+3\beta\phi)}s_1 \\
& +\frac{1}{4}\phi\frac{6\beta\delta[\alpha\delta+\varepsilon(1-\gamma)]-\varepsilon[(1-\gamma)(1+2\gamma)]-2\alpha[(\delta+\phi)(1+2\gamma)]+3\beta\phi[2\alpha\delta+\varepsilon(1-\gamma)]}{(\delta+\phi)[\alpha(\delta+\phi)+\varepsilon(1-\gamma)](1+2\gamma+3\beta\phi)}s_2 \\
& -\frac{1}{2}\frac{\varepsilon(1-\gamma)}{(\delta+\phi)[\alpha(\delta+\phi)+\varepsilon(1-\gamma)]}m^*+\frac{1}{2}\frac{\varepsilon}{[\alpha(\delta+\phi)+\varepsilon(1-\gamma)]}f^*+\frac{1}{2}\phi\frac{\varepsilon(1-\gamma)}{(\delta+\phi)[\alpha(\delta+\phi)+\varepsilon(1-\gamma)]}s^* \\
& +\frac{1}{4}\frac{\varepsilon(1-\gamma)(1-2(\sigma+\sigma'))-2\alpha(\sigma+\sigma')(\delta+\phi)}{(\delta+\phi)[\alpha(\delta+\phi)+\varepsilon(1-\gamma)]}(p_{1,-1}+p_{2,-1}) \\
& -\frac{1}{2}\frac{\varepsilon(1-\gamma)(1-2(\sigma+\sigma'))-2\alpha(1-\sigma-\sigma')(\delta+\phi)}{(\delta+\phi)[\alpha(\delta+\phi)+\varepsilon(1-\gamma)]}p^*_{-1}-\frac{(1-\sigma-\sigma')}{(\delta+\phi)}e_{-1}
\end{aligned}
$$

$$
\begin{aligned}
y_2 = {} & \frac{1}{2}\frac{\varepsilon(1-\gamma)+2\alpha(\delta+\phi)}{(\delta+\phi)[\alpha(\delta+\phi)+\varepsilon(1-\gamma)]}m-\frac{1}{4}\frac{2\alpha(\delta+\phi)+\varepsilon(1-4\gamma-3\beta\phi)}{[\alpha(\delta+\phi)+\varepsilon(1-\gamma)](1+2\gamma+3\beta\phi)}f_1+\frac{1}{4}\frac{2\alpha(\delta+\phi)+3\varepsilon(1+\beta\phi)}{[\alpha(\delta+\phi)+\varepsilon(1-\gamma)](1+2\gamma+3\beta\phi)}f_2 \\
& +\frac{1}{4}\phi\frac{6\beta\delta[\alpha\delta+\varepsilon(1-\gamma)]-\varepsilon[(1-\gamma)(1+2\gamma)]-2\alpha[(\delta+\phi)(1+2\gamma)]+3\beta\phi[2\alpha\delta+\varepsilon(1-\gamma)]}{(\delta+\phi)[\alpha(\delta+\phi)+\varepsilon(1-\gamma)](1+2\gamma+3\beta\phi)}s_1 \\
& -\frac{1}{4}\phi\frac{6\beta\delta[\alpha\delta+\varepsilon(1-\gamma)]+\varepsilon[(1-\gamma)(1+2\gamma)]+2\alpha[(\delta+\phi)(1+2\gamma)]+9\beta\phi[2\alpha\delta+\varepsilon(1-\gamma)]+12\alpha\beta\phi^2}{(\delta+\phi)[\alpha(\delta+\phi)+\varepsilon(1-\gamma)](1+2\gamma+3\beta\phi)}s_2 \\
& -\frac{1}{2}\frac{\varepsilon(1-\gamma)}{(\delta+\phi)[\alpha(\delta+\phi)+\varepsilon(1-\gamma)]}m^*+\frac{1}{2}\frac{\varepsilon}{[\alpha(\delta+\phi)+\varepsilon(1-\gamma)]}f^*+\frac{1}{2}\phi\frac{\varepsilon(1-\gamma)}{(\delta+\phi)[\alpha(\delta+\phi)+\varepsilon(1-\gamma)]}s^* \\
& +\frac{1}{4}\frac{\varepsilon(1-\gamma)(1-2(\sigma+\sigma'))-2\alpha(\sigma+\sigma')(\delta+\phi)}{(\delta+\phi)[\alpha(\delta+\phi)+\varepsilon(1-\gamma)]}(p_{1,-1}+p_{2,-1}) \\
& -\frac{1}{2}\frac{\varepsilon(1-\gamma)(1-2(\sigma+\sigma'))-2\alpha(1-\sigma-\sigma')(\delta+\phi)}{(\delta+\phi)[\alpha(\delta+\phi)+\varepsilon(1-\gamma)]}p^*_{-1}-\frac{(1-\sigma-\sigma')}{(\delta+\phi)}e_{-1}
\end{aligned}
$$

$$
\begin{aligned}
p_1 = {} & \frac{1}{2}\phi\frac{\varepsilon(1-\gamma)+2\alpha(\delta+\phi)}{(\delta+\phi)[\alpha(\delta+\phi)+\varepsilon(1-\gamma)]}m+\frac{1}{4}\phi\frac{2\alpha(\delta+\phi)+\varepsilon(3+\beta\phi)}{[\alpha(\delta+\phi)+\varepsilon(1-\gamma)](1+2\gamma+3\beta\phi)}f_1-\frac{1}{4}\phi\frac{2\alpha(\delta+\phi)+\varepsilon(1-4\gamma-3\beta\phi)}{[\alpha(\delta+\phi)+\varepsilon(1-\gamma)](1+2\gamma+3\beta\phi)}f_2 \\
& -\frac{1}{4}\phi\frac{6\beta\delta\phi[\alpha\delta+\varepsilon(1-\gamma)]+3\varepsilon\phi[(1-\gamma)(1+2\gamma)]+3\beta\phi^2[2\alpha\delta+\varepsilon(1-\gamma)]+2\alpha(1+2\gamma)\left[\delta(3\phi+2\delta)+\phi^2\right]+4\delta\varepsilon(1-\gamma)(1-2\gamma)}{(\delta+\phi)[\alpha(\delta+\phi)+\varepsilon(1-\gamma)](1+2\gamma+3\beta\phi)}s_1 \\
& -\frac{1}{4}\phi^2\frac{6\beta\delta[\alpha\delta+\varepsilon(1-\gamma)]-\varepsilon[(1-\gamma)(1+2\gamma)]-2\alpha[(\delta+\phi)(1+2\gamma)]+3\beta\phi[2\alpha\delta+\varepsilon(1-\gamma)]}{(\delta+\phi)[\alpha(\delta+\phi)+\varepsilon(1-\gamma)](1+2\gamma+3\beta\phi)}s_2 \\
& -\frac{1}{2}\phi\frac{\varepsilon(1-\gamma)}{(\delta+\phi)[\alpha(\delta+\phi)+\varepsilon(1-\gamma)]}m^*+\frac{1}{2}\phi\frac{\varepsilon}{[\alpha(\delta+\phi)+\varepsilon(1-\gamma)]}f^*+\frac{1}{2}\phi\frac{\varepsilon\phi(1-\gamma)}{(\delta+\phi)[\alpha(\delta+\phi)+\varepsilon(1-\gamma)]}s^* \\
& +\frac{1}{4}\frac{2\delta(\sigma+\sigma')[\alpha(\delta+\phi)+\varepsilon(1-\gamma)]+\varepsilon\phi(1-\gamma)}{(\delta+\phi)[\alpha(\delta+\phi)+\varepsilon(1-\gamma)]}p_{1,-1}+\frac{1}{4}\frac{2\delta(1-\sigma+\sigma')[\alpha(\delta+\phi)+\varepsilon(1-\gamma)]+\varepsilon\phi(1-\gamma)}{(\delta+\phi)[\alpha(\delta+\phi)+\varepsilon(1-\gamma)]}p_{2,-1} \\
& -\frac{1}{2}\frac{2\delta(1-\sigma-\sigma')[\alpha(\delta+\phi)+\varepsilon(1-\gamma)]+\varepsilon\phi(1-\gamma)}{(\delta+\phi)[\alpha(\delta+\phi)+\varepsilon(1-\gamma)]}p^*_{-1}-\frac{\delta(1-\sigma-\sigma')}{(\delta+\phi)}e_{-1}
\end{aligned}
$$

$$
\begin{aligned}
p_2 = {} & \frac{1}{2}\phi\frac{\varepsilon(1-\gamma)+2\alpha(\delta+\phi)}{(\delta+\phi)[\alpha(\delta+\phi)+\varepsilon(1-\gamma)]}m-\frac{1}{4}\phi\frac{2\alpha(\delta+\phi)+\varepsilon(1-4\gamma-3\beta\phi)}{[\alpha(\delta+\phi)+\varepsilon(1-\gamma)](1+2\gamma+3\beta\phi)}f_1+\frac{1}{4}\phi\frac{2\alpha(\delta+\phi)+\varepsilon(3+\beta\phi)}{[\alpha(\delta+\phi)+\varepsilon(1-\gamma)](1+2\gamma+3\beta\phi)}f_2 \\
& -\frac{1}{4}\phi^2\frac{6\beta\delta[\alpha\delta+\varepsilon(1-\gamma)]-\varepsilon[(1-\gamma)(1+2\gamma)]-2\alpha[(\delta+\phi)(1+2\gamma)]+3\beta\phi[2\alpha\delta+\varepsilon(1-\gamma)]}{(\delta+\phi)[\alpha(\delta+\phi)+\varepsilon(1-\gamma)](1+2\gamma+3\beta\phi)}s_1 \\
& -\frac{1}{4}\phi\frac{6\beta\delta\phi[\alpha\delta+\varepsilon(1-\gamma)]+3\varepsilon\phi[(1-\gamma)(1+2\gamma)]+3\beta\phi^2[2\alpha\delta+\varepsilon(1-\gamma)]+2\alpha(1+2\gamma)\left[\delta(3\phi+2\delta)+\phi^2\right]+4\delta\varepsilon(1-\gamma)(1-2\gamma)}{(\delta+\phi)[\alpha(\delta+\phi)+\varepsilon(1-\gamma)](1+2\gamma+3\beta\phi)}s_2 \\
& -\frac{1}{2}\phi\frac{\varepsilon(1-\gamma)}{(\delta+\phi)[\alpha(\delta+\phi)+\varepsilon(1-\gamma)]}m^*+\frac{1}{2}\phi\frac{\varepsilon}{[\alpha(\delta+\phi)+\varepsilon(1-\gamma)]}f^*+\frac{1}{2}\phi\frac{\varepsilon\phi(1-\gamma)}{(\delta+\phi)[\alpha(\delta+\phi)+\varepsilon(1-\gamma)]}s^* \\
& +\frac{1}{4}\frac{2\delta(\sigma+\sigma')[\alpha(\delta+\phi)+\varepsilon(1-\gamma)]+\varepsilon\phi(1-\gamma)}{(\delta+\phi)[\alpha(\delta+\phi)+\varepsilon(1-\gamma)]}p_{1,-1}+\frac{1}{4}\frac{2\delta(1-\sigma+\sigma')[\alpha(\delta+\phi)+\varepsilon(1-\gamma)]+\varepsilon\phi(1-\gamma)}{(\delta+\phi)[\alpha(\delta+\phi)+\varepsilon(1-\gamma)]}p_{2,-1} \\
& -\frac{1}{2}\frac{2\delta(1-\sigma-\sigma')[\alpha(\delta+\phi)+\varepsilon(1-\gamma)]+\varepsilon\phi(1-\gamma)}{(\delta+\phi)[\alpha(\delta+\phi)+\varepsilon(1-\gamma)]}p^*_{-1}-\frac{\delta(1-\sigma-\sigma')}{(\delta+\phi)}e_{-1}
\end{aligned}
$$

$$
\begin{aligned}
e = {} & \frac{1}{2}\frac{(1+\gamma)+2\beta\phi}{\beta(\phi+\delta)}m-\frac{1}{4\beta}f_1-\frac{1}{4\beta}f_2-\frac{1}{4}\frac{\phi[(1+\gamma)-2\beta\delta]}{\beta(\phi+\delta)}(s_1+s_2) \\
& -\frac{1}{2}\frac{(1+\gamma)+2\beta\phi}{\beta(\phi+\delta)}m^*+\frac{1}{2\beta}f^*+\frac{1}{2}\frac{\phi[(1+\gamma)-2\beta\delta]}{\beta(\phi+\delta)}s^* \\
& +\frac{1}{4}\frac{[1-2(\sigma+\sigma')][(1+\gamma)-2\beta\delta]}{\beta(\phi+\delta)}(p_{1,-1}+p_{2,-1}) \\
& -\frac{1}{2}\frac{[1-2(\sigma+\sigma')][(1+\gamma)-2\beta\delta]}{\beta(\phi+\delta)}p^*_{-1}-\frac{(1-\sigma-\sigma')[(1+\gamma)-2\beta\delta]}{\beta(\phi+\delta)}e_{-1}
\end{aligned}
$$

$$
\begin{aligned}
y^* = & -\frac{1}{2}\frac{(1-\gamma)}{(\phi+\delta)[\alpha(\phi+\delta)+\varepsilon(1-\gamma)]}m + \frac{1}{4}\frac{\varepsilon}{[\alpha(\phi+\delta)+\varepsilon(1-\gamma)]}f_1 \\
& + \frac{1}{4}\frac{\varepsilon}{[\alpha(\phi+\delta)+(1-\gamma)]}f_2 + \frac{1}{4}\frac{\varepsilon\phi(1-\gamma)}{(\phi+\delta)[\alpha(\phi+\delta)+\varepsilon(1-\gamma)]}s_1 \\
& + \frac{1}{4}\frac{\varepsilon\phi(1-\gamma)}{(\phi+\delta)[\alpha(\phi+\delta)+\varepsilon(1-\gamma)]}s_2 + \frac{1}{2}\frac{2\alpha(\phi+\delta)+\varepsilon(1-\gamma)}{(\phi+\delta)[\alpha(\phi+\delta)+\varepsilon(1-\gamma)]}m^* \\
& + \frac{1}{2}\frac{\varepsilon}{[\alpha(\phi+\delta)+\varepsilon(1-\gamma)]}f^* - \frac{1}{2}\phi\frac{\varepsilon(1-\gamma)+2\alpha(\phi+\delta)}{[\phi+\delta][\alpha(\phi+\delta)+\varepsilon(1-\gamma)]}s^* \\
& + \frac{1}{4}\frac{\varepsilon(1-\gamma)(\sigma+\sigma')-\alpha(\phi+\delta)(1-\sigma-\sigma')}{(\phi+\delta)[\alpha(\phi+\delta)+\varepsilon(1-\gamma)]}(p_{1,-1}+p_{2,-1}) \\
& - \frac{1}{2}\frac{\varepsilon(1-\gamma)[1-2(\sigma+\sigma')]-2\alpha(\sigma+\sigma')(\phi+\delta)}{(\phi+\delta)[\alpha(\phi+\delta)+\varepsilon(1-\gamma)]}p^*_{-1} - \frac{(1-\sigma-\sigma')}{(\phi+\delta)}e_{-1}
\end{aligned}
$$

$$
\begin{aligned}
p^* = & -\frac{1}{2}\frac{\varepsilon\phi(1-\gamma)}{(\phi+\delta)[\alpha(\phi+\delta)+\varepsilon(1-\gamma)]}m + \frac{1}{4}\frac{\phi\varepsilon}{[\alpha(\phi+\delta)+\varepsilon(1-\gamma)]}f_1 \\
& + \frac{1}{4}\frac{\phi\varepsilon}{[\alpha(\phi+\delta)+(1-\gamma)]}f_2 + \frac{1}{4}\frac{\varepsilon\phi^2(1-\gamma)}{(\phi+\delta)[\alpha(\phi+\delta)+\varepsilon(1-\gamma)]}s_1 \\
& + \frac{1}{4}\frac{\varepsilon\phi^2(1-\gamma)}{(\phi+\delta)[\alpha(\phi+\delta)+\varepsilon(1-\gamma)]}s_2 + \frac{1}{2}\phi\frac{2\alpha(\phi+\delta)+\varepsilon(1-\gamma)}{(\phi+\delta)[\alpha(\phi+\delta)+\varepsilon(1-\gamma)]}m^* \\
& + \frac{1}{2}\frac{\phi\varepsilon}{[\alpha(\phi+\delta)+\varepsilon(1-\gamma)]}f^* + \frac{1}{2}\frac{\varepsilon\phi^2(1-\gamma)+2\delta\phi[\alpha(\phi+\delta)+\varepsilon(1-\gamma)]}{[\phi+\delta][\alpha(\phi+\delta)+\varepsilon(1-\gamma)]}s^* \\
& + \frac{1}{4}\frac{\varepsilon\phi(1-\gamma)+2\delta(1-\sigma-\sigma')[\alpha(\phi+\delta)+\varepsilon(1-\gamma)]}{(\phi+\delta)[\alpha(\phi+\delta)+\varepsilon(1-\gamma)]}(p_{1,-1}+p_{2,-1}) \\
& + \frac{1}{2}\frac{\varepsilon\phi(1-\gamma)+2\delta(\sigma+\sigma')[\alpha(\phi+\delta)+\varepsilon(1-\gamma)]}{(\phi+\delta)[\alpha(\phi+\delta)+\varepsilon(1-\gamma)]}p^*_{-1} - \frac{\delta(1-\sigma-\sigma')}{(\phi+\delta)}e_{-1}
\end{aligned}
$$

$$
\begin{aligned}
i^* = & -\frac{1}{2}\frac{(1-\gamma)}{[\alpha(\phi+\delta)+\varepsilon(1-\gamma)]}m + \frac{1}{4}\frac{(\delta+\phi)}{[\alpha(\phi+\delta)+\varepsilon(1-\gamma)]}f_1 \\
& + \frac{1}{4}\frac{(\delta+\phi)}{[\alpha(\phi+\delta)+(1-\gamma)]}f_2 + \frac{1}{4}\frac{\phi(1-\gamma)}{[\alpha(\phi+\delta)+\varepsilon(1-\gamma)]}s_1 \\
& + \frac{1}{4}\frac{\phi(1-\gamma)}{[\alpha(\phi+\delta)+\varepsilon(1-\gamma)]}s_2 - \frac{1}{2}\frac{(1-\gamma)}{[\alpha(\phi+\delta)+\varepsilon(1-\gamma)]}m^* \\
& + \frac{1}{2}\frac{(\delta+\phi)}{[\alpha(\phi+\delta)+\varepsilon(1-\gamma)]}f^* + \frac{1}{2}\phi\frac{(1-\gamma)}{[\alpha(\phi+\delta)+\varepsilon(1-\gamma)]}s^* \\
& + \frac{1}{4}\frac{(1-\gamma)}{[\alpha(\phi+\delta)+\varepsilon(1-\gamma)]}(p_{1,-1}+p_{2,-1}) + \frac{1}{2}\frac{(1-\gamma)}{[\alpha(\phi+\delta)+\varepsilon(1-\gamma)]}p^*_{-1}
\end{aligned}
$$

Long Run

$$y_1 = \frac{1}{4}\frac{(1-\sigma-\sigma')(1-\sigma+\sigma')(3+4\gamma)+\beta\phi(5-5\sigma-\sigma')}{[(1+\gamma)(1-\sigma-\sigma')+\beta\phi][(1+2\gamma)(1-\sigma+\sigma')+3\beta\phi]}f_1 - \frac{1}{4}\frac{(1-\sigma-\sigma')(1-\sigma+\sigma')-\beta\phi(1-\sigma-5\sigma')}{[(1+\gamma)(1-\sigma-\sigma')+\beta\phi][(1+2\gamma)(1-\sigma+\sigma')+3\beta\phi]}f_2$$

$$-\frac{1}{4}\frac{(1+\gamma)(1+2\gamma)(1-\sigma-\sigma')(1-\sigma+\sigma')+\beta\phi(11-11\sigma-7\sigma')+\gamma\beta\phi(13-13\sigma-5\sigma')+12\beta^2\phi^2}{[(1+\gamma)(1-\sigma-\sigma')+\beta\phi][(1+2\gamma)(1-\sigma+\sigma')+3\beta\phi]}s_1$$

$$-\frac{1}{4}\frac{(1+\gamma)(1+2\gamma)(1-\sigma-\sigma')(1-\sigma+\sigma')-\beta\phi(1-\sigma-5\sigma')+\gamma\beta\phi(1-\sigma+7\sigma')}{[(1+\gamma)(1-\sigma-\sigma')+\beta\phi][(1+2\gamma)(1-\sigma+\sigma')+3\beta\phi]}s_2$$

$$-\frac{1}{2}\frac{(1-\sigma-\sigma')}{[(1+\gamma)(1-\sigma-\sigma')+\beta\phi]}f^* - \frac{1}{2}\frac{(1+\gamma)(1-\sigma-\sigma')}{[(1+\gamma)(1-\sigma-\sigma')+\beta\phi]}s^*$$

$$y_2 = -\frac{1}{4}\frac{(1-\sigma-\sigma')(1-\sigma+\sigma')-\beta\phi(1-\sigma-5\sigma')}{[(1+\gamma)(1-\sigma-\sigma')+\beta\phi][(1+2\gamma)(1-\sigma+\sigma')+3\beta\phi]}f_1$$

$$+\frac{1}{4}\frac{(1-\sigma-\sigma')(1-\sigma+\sigma')(3+4\gamma)+\beta\phi(5-5\sigma-\sigma')}{[(1+\gamma)(1-\sigma-\sigma')+\beta\phi][(1+2\gamma)(1-\sigma+\sigma')+3\beta\phi]}f_2$$

$$-\frac{1}{4}\frac{(1+\gamma)(1+2\gamma)(1-\sigma-\sigma')(1-\sigma+\sigma')-\beta\phi(1-\sigma-5\sigma')+\gamma\beta\phi(1-\sigma+7\sigma')}{[(1+\gamma)(1-\sigma-\sigma')+\beta\phi][(1+2\gamma)(1-\sigma+\sigma')+3\beta\phi]}s_1$$

$$-\frac{1}{4}\frac{(1+\gamma)(1+2\gamma)(1-\sigma-\sigma')(1-\sigma+\sigma')+\beta\phi(11-11\sigma-7\sigma')+\gamma\beta\phi(13-13\sigma-5\sigma')+12\beta^2\phi^2}{[(1+\gamma)(1-\sigma-\sigma')+\beta\phi][(1+2\gamma)(1-\sigma+\sigma')+3\beta\phi]}s_2$$

$$-\frac{1}{2}\frac{(1-\sigma-\sigma')}{[(1+\gamma)(1-\sigma-\sigma')+\beta\phi]}f^* - \frac{1}{2}\frac{(1+\gamma)(1-\sigma-\sigma')}{[(1+\gamma)(1-\sigma-\sigma')+\beta\phi]}s^*$$

$$p_1 = m + \frac{1}{4}\frac{[\varepsilon[(1-\sigma-\sigma')(1+\gamma)+\beta\phi]-\delta\alpha(1-\sigma-\sigma')][(1-\sigma+\sigma')(1+2\gamma)+3\beta\phi]+2\phi\alpha[(1-\sigma-\sigma')(1+\gamma)+\beta\phi]}{\alpha[(1-\sigma-\sigma')(1+\gamma)+\beta\phi](1-\sigma+\sigma')(1+2\gamma)+3\beta\phi}f_1$$

$$+\frac{1}{4}\frac{[\varepsilon[(1-\sigma-\sigma')(1+\gamma)+\beta\phi]-\delta\alpha(1-\sigma-\sigma')][(1-\sigma+\sigma')(1+2\gamma)+3\beta\phi]-2\phi\alpha[(1-\sigma-\sigma')(1+\gamma)+\beta\phi]}{\alpha[(1-\sigma-\sigma')(1+\gamma)+\beta\phi](1-\sigma+\sigma')(1+2\gamma)+3\beta\phi}f_2$$

$$+\frac{1}{4}\frac{[(1-\gamma)\varepsilon[(1-\sigma-\sigma')(1+\gamma)+\beta\phi]+\alpha\delta[(1+\gamma)(1-\sigma-\sigma')+2\beta\phi]][(1-\sigma+\sigma')(1+2\gamma)+3\beta\phi]+2(1+2\gamma)\phi\alpha[(1-\sigma-\sigma')(1+\gamma)+\beta\phi]}{\alpha[(1-\sigma-\sigma')(1+\gamma)+\beta\phi](1-\sigma+\sigma')(1+2\gamma)+3\beta\phi}s_1$$

$$+\frac{1}{4}\frac{[(1-\gamma)\varepsilon[(1-\sigma-\sigma')(1+\gamma)+\beta\phi]+\alpha\delta[(1+\gamma)(1-\sigma-\sigma')+2\beta\phi]][(1-\sigma+\sigma')(1+2\gamma)+3\beta\phi]-2(1+2\gamma)\phi\alpha[(1-\sigma-\sigma')(1+\gamma)+\beta\phi]}{\alpha[(1-\sigma-\sigma')(1+\gamma)+\beta\phi](1-\sigma+\sigma')(1+2\gamma)+3\beta\phi}s_2$$

$$+\frac{1}{2}\frac{[\varepsilon[(1-\sigma-\sigma')(1+\gamma)+\beta\phi]-\alpha\delta(1-\sigma-\sigma')]}{\alpha[(1-\sigma-\sigma')(1+\gamma)+\beta\phi](1-\sigma+\sigma')(1+2\gamma)+3\beta\phi}f^* + \frac{1}{2}\frac{[(1-\gamma)\varepsilon[(1-\sigma-\sigma')(1+\gamma)+\beta\phi]+\alpha\delta[(1+\gamma)(1-\sigma-\sigma')]]}{\alpha[(1-\sigma-\sigma')(1+\gamma)+\beta\phi](1-\sigma+\sigma')(1+2\gamma)+3\beta\phi}s^*$$

$$p_2 = m + \frac{1}{4}\frac{[\varepsilon[(1-\sigma-\sigma')(1+\gamma)+\beta\phi]-\delta\alpha(1-\sigma-\sigma')][(1-\sigma+\sigma')(1+2\gamma)+3\beta\phi]-2\phi\alpha[(1-\sigma-\sigma')(1+\gamma)+\beta\phi]}{\alpha[(1-\sigma-\sigma')(1+\gamma)+\beta\phi](1-\sigma+\sigma')(1+2\gamma)+3\beta\phi}f_1$$

$$+\frac{1}{4}\frac{[\varepsilon[(1-\sigma-\sigma')(1+\gamma)+\beta\phi]-\delta\alpha(1-\sigma-\sigma')][(1-\sigma+\sigma')(1+2\gamma)+3\beta\phi]+2\phi\alpha[(1-\sigma-\sigma')(1+\gamma)+\beta\phi]}{\alpha[(1-\sigma-\sigma')(1+\gamma)+\beta\phi](1-\sigma+\sigma')(1+2\gamma)+3\beta\phi}f_2$$

$$+\frac{1}{4}\frac{[(1-\gamma)\varepsilon[(1-\sigma-\sigma')(1+\gamma)+\beta\phi]+\alpha\delta[(1+\gamma)(1-\sigma-\sigma')+2\beta\phi]][(1-\sigma+\sigma')(1+2\gamma)+3\beta\phi]-2(1+2\gamma)\phi\alpha[(1-\sigma-\sigma')(1+\gamma)+\beta\phi]}{\alpha[(1-\sigma-\sigma')(1+\gamma)+\beta\phi](1-\sigma+\sigma')(1+2\gamma)+3\beta\phi}s_1$$

$$+\frac{1}{4}\frac{[(1-\gamma)\varepsilon[(1-\sigma-\sigma')(1+\gamma)+\beta\phi]+\alpha\delta[(1+\gamma)(1-\sigma-\sigma')+2\beta\phi]][(1-\sigma+\sigma')(1+2\gamma)+3\beta\phi]+2(1+2\gamma)\phi\alpha[(1-\sigma-\sigma')(1+\gamma)+\beta\phi]}{\alpha[(1-\sigma-\sigma')(1+\gamma)+\beta\phi](1-\sigma+\sigma')(1+2\gamma)+3\beta\phi}s_2$$

$$+\frac{1}{2}\frac{[\varepsilon[(1-\sigma-\sigma')(1+\gamma)+\beta\phi]-\alpha\delta(1-\sigma-\sigma')]}{\alpha[(1-\sigma-\sigma')(1+\gamma)+\beta\phi](1-\sigma+\sigma')(1+2\gamma)+3\beta\phi}f^* + \frac{1}{2}\frac{[(1-\gamma)\varepsilon[(1-\sigma-\sigma')(1+\gamma)+\beta\phi]+\alpha\delta[(1+\gamma)(1-\sigma-\sigma')]]}{\alpha[(1-\sigma-\sigma')(1+\gamma)+\beta\phi](1-\sigma+\sigma')(1+2\gamma)+3\beta\phi}s^*$$

$$e = m - \frac{1}{4}\frac{\phi + 2\delta(1-\sigma-\sigma')}{(1+\gamma)(1-\sigma-\sigma')+\beta\phi}f_1 - \frac{1}{4}\frac{\phi + 2\delta(1-\sigma-\sigma')}{(1+\gamma)(1-\sigma-\sigma')+\beta\phi}f_2$$
$$-\frac{1}{4}\phi\frac{(1+\gamma)-2\beta\phi}{(1+\gamma)(1-\sigma-\sigma')+\beta\phi}s_1 - \phi\frac{1}{4}\frac{(1+\gamma)-2\beta\phi}{(1+\gamma)(1-\sigma-\sigma')+\beta\phi}s_2 - m^*$$
$$+\frac{1}{2}\frac{\phi + 2\delta(1-\sigma-\sigma')}{(1+\gamma)(1-\sigma-\sigma')+\beta\phi}f^* + \frac{1}{2}\phi\frac{(1+\gamma)-2\beta\phi}{(1+\gamma)(1-\sigma-\sigma')+\beta\phi}s^*$$

$$y^* = -\frac{1}{4}\frac{(1-\sigma-\sigma')}{[(1+\gamma)(1-\sigma-\sigma')+\beta\phi]}f_1 - \frac{1}{4}\frac{(1-\sigma-\sigma')}{[(1+\gamma)(1-\sigma-\sigma')+\beta\phi]}f_2$$
$$-\frac{1}{4}\frac{(1+\gamma)(1-\sigma-\sigma')}{[(1+\gamma)(1-\sigma-\sigma')+\beta\phi]}s_1 - \frac{1}{4}\frac{(1+\gamma)(1-\sigma-\sigma')}{[(1+\gamma)(1-\sigma-\sigma')+\beta\phi]}s_2$$
$$+\frac{1}{2}\frac{(1-\sigma-\sigma')}{[(1+\gamma)(1-\sigma-\sigma')+\beta\phi]}f^* - \frac{1}{2}\frac{(1+\gamma)(1-\sigma-\sigma')+2\beta\phi}{[(1+\gamma)(1-\sigma-\sigma')+\beta\phi]}s^*$$

$$p^* = \frac{1}{4}\frac{[\varepsilon[(1-\sigma-\sigma')(1+\gamma)+\beta\phi]+\alpha\delta(1-\sigma-\sigma')]}{\alpha[(1-\sigma-\sigma')(1+\gamma)+\beta\phi]}f_1$$
$$+\frac{1}{4}\frac{[\varepsilon[(1-\sigma-\sigma')(1+\gamma)+\beta\phi]+\alpha\delta(1-\sigma-\sigma')]}{\alpha[(1-\sigma-\sigma')(1+\gamma)+\beta\phi]}f_2$$
$$+\frac{1}{4}\frac{[(1-\gamma)\varepsilon[(1-\sigma-\sigma')(1+\gamma)+\beta\phi]+\alpha\delta[(1+\gamma)(1-\sigma-\sigma')]]}{\alpha[(1-\sigma-\sigma')(1+\gamma)+\beta\phi]}s_1$$
$$+\frac{1}{4}\frac{[(1-\gamma)\varepsilon[(1-\sigma-\sigma')(1+\gamma)+\beta\phi]+\alpha\delta[(1+\gamma)(1-\sigma-\sigma')]]}{\alpha[(1-\sigma-\sigma')(1+\gamma)+\beta\phi]}s_2 + m^*$$
$$+\frac{1}{2}\frac{[\varepsilon[(1-\sigma-\sigma')(1+\gamma)+\beta\phi]-\alpha\delta(1-\sigma-\sigma')]}{\alpha[(1-\sigma-\sigma')(1+\gamma)+\beta\phi]}f^*$$
$$+\frac{1}{2}\frac{[(1-\gamma)\varepsilon[(1-\sigma-\sigma')(1+\gamma)+\beta\phi]+\alpha\delta[(1+\gamma)(1-\sigma-\sigma')+2\beta\phi]]}{\alpha[(1-\sigma-\sigma')(1+\gamma)+\beta\phi]}s^*$$

$$i^* = \frac{1}{4\alpha}f_1 + \frac{1}{4\alpha}f_2 + \frac{(1-\gamma)}{4\alpha}s_1 + \frac{(1-\gamma)}{4\alpha}s_2 + \frac{1}{2\alpha}f^* + \frac{(1-\gamma)}{2\alpha}s^*$$